CW01083383

SO YOU THINK YOU KNOW ABOUT THE HOLY ROYAL ARCH?

RAY HUDSON

First published 2015
Copyright © 2015 Aziloth Books

Every effort has been made to contact all copyright holders. The publisher will be glad to make good in future editions any errors or omissions brought to their attention.

This publication is designed to provide authoritative and accurate information in regard to the subject matter covered. It is sold on the understanding that the Publisher is not engaged in rendering professional services.

British Library Cataloguing in Publication Data

A catalogue record for this book is available from the British Library

ISBN-13: 978-1-909735-74-3

Printed and bound in Great Britain by Lightning Source UK Ltd., 6 Precedent Drive, Rooksley, Milton Keynes MK13 8PR.

Cover Illustration: The Triple Tau of the Holy Royal Arch

ACKNOWLEGEMENTS

No real achievement can be obtained without a great deal of assistance, no matter how subtle that assistance may be, and this book is no exception to that claim.

My thanks go out to all my close Masonic friends who have patiently listened to my theories, debated and guided me as we travelled to various meetings. Also the many papers and books that I have collected over many years of research, and of course the Web, that "tool" that can be as equally misleading as it can be a guide, but one soon learns to be selective.

But I simply must acknowledge my original Masonic Mentor who, in the very early years, guided and encouraged me in research and in lecturing. He was my Director of Ceremonies and extremely knowledgeable in many degrees of Freemasonry. A gentle and great man, who in his dying years would still exchange views and correct me from his sick bed. A loss I still feel and it is to him that I owe a great deal and I fully acknowledge that. His name, for the record was W.B.John Hoy. He was fully responsible for encouraging me into many of the so-called side Orders within Freemasonry, and I still wear some of his regalia that his wife passed on to me after his demise. He certainly lived respected and died regretted.

My thanks. As usual, go to my publisher and friend Keith Laidler, founder of Aziloth Books and a great researcher and writer in his own right.

How fortunate I am to know and have known such people. I am indebted to them all.

My biggest debt is to Freemasonry itself, a wonderful institution that has given me so much over the last 30 or so years.

Ray Hudson

February 2015

CONTENTS

CHAPTER 1	THE BEGINNING	9
CHAPTER2	"OUR GREAT AND ILLUSTRIOUS FOUNDER"	11
CHAPTER 3	EGYPT AT THE TIME OF MOSES	16
CHAPTER 4	BIBLICAL REFERENCES TO EGYPT	22
CHAPTER 5	TWO CANDIDATES FOR CREATING MONOTHEISM	31
CHAPTER 6	MOSES.... THE STORY CONTINUES	38
CHAPTER 7	THE ROD OF AARON/MOSES	46
CHAPTER 8	THE EXODUS.	52
CHAPTER 9	AHKENATEN	56
CHAPTER 10	THE HOLY ROYAL ARCH.	62
CHAPTER 11	THE CAST	67
CHAPTER 12	THE ENSIGNS OF THE TWELVE TRIBES	80
CHAPTER 13	JEHOVAH	100
CHAPTER 14	THE THREE SOJOURNERS	103
CHAPTER 15	COMPLETION BY NUMBERS	106
CHAPTER 16	THE CONTINUANCE BY NUMBERS	108
CHAPTER 17	THE EXALTATION CEREMONY	111
CHAPTER 18	CONCLUSION, & THE JOURNEY CONTINUES	118

INTRODUCTION

Due to the unprecedented success of my previous book, *So You Think You Know About Freemasonry*, where I detailed the history, ritual and symbolism of the Craft, as I see it, again I have been inundated with requests to do the same for the Holy Royal Arch, or as it is more familiarly referred to, The Chapter. The Holy Royal Arch is generally regarded to be the next natural step once you become a Master Mason. I say generally but it is not always the case. The chronology of the Masonic Orders is out of sync with the history that it is structured to portray. This is due to a couple of reasons. First, that the United Grand Lodge of England governs the Craft and also determines the policies of the Supreme Grand Chapter who governs the Holy Royal Arch, therefore strong encouragement is given to Master Masons of the Craft to join the Chapter once they have been a Master Mason for 4 weeks and upwards. Secondly, that the Mark Degree and the majority of the other mainstream Masonic Orders are governed by Mark Masons Hall. Although both governing bodies have a great appreciation for each other, so far they have not come that closely together in order to solve the synchronisation of the chronological imperfections that exist between the various Masonic Orders. To give the obvious example; between the Master Masons degree of the Craft, which is a degree portraying a loss, in that the ability to communicate the Master word forms the loss as well as that of the death of one the three Grand Masters, as those three were the only ones that were able to communicate the Master word, and the degree of the Holy Royal Arch, which is a degree portraying a discovery, that being the finding of the method of communicating the Master Word, between these two important events there is a gap of 470 years. As the majority of the Masonic Orders portray events in Judaic history, culture and religion, there is much explored within Freemasonry that occurred within the aforementioned 470 year period, which is fully explored in many other fully recognised Masonic Orders. The very popular Mark Master Masons degree takes its provenance from the Craft 2nd Degree, which is chronologically correct as originally there were only 2 degrees within the Craft in the very early years. There are many Masonic Orders that aid in the "filling in" of those 470 years and therefore add greatly to the understanding of the Craft and the Holy Royal Arch. As I have mentioned before, if you buy a book and only read chapters 1 & 2, then the rest of the book is lost to you, so the full understanding and appreciation of the complete story and its complete objectives is also lost to you. Of course a great enjoyment and satisfaction can be obtained by only being a member of the Craft and the Holy Royal Arch, and there are many Masons that achieve such satisfaction. But how much more can be obtained by delving further into the allegorical book of Freemasonry by being selective in which path you wish to pursue within your Masonic career. Careful contemplation and consideration is therefore highly recommended. Being avid in my pursuit for complete Masonic knowledge and awareness, I have been and am a member of every recognised Masonic Order. Studied each one, researched each one, lectured in each one. I have gained immense amounts of knowledge, history, plus awareness and understanding of myself which has proved to be so beneficial that words could not possibly do justice for. I am still actively pursuing my Masonic path and doubt that I will ever reach the rainbow at the end. But the journey itself is thoroughly worth the effort and time.

Once again my researches are so varied and many that to detail them would take a book on its own, so please excuse the lack of a bibliography.

Again I have kept the explanations fairly basic and have left the personal interpretations intact, as they are precisely that and should be left to the individual.

As well as being an active member of the Holy Royal Arch in West Kent, I am also a life member of a Scottish Chapter in Edinburgh, (Canongate & Kilwinning No. 56), and therefore have the distinct advantage of two aspects of the portrayal of this story of discovery. Furthermore I am a member of several other Masonic Orders that specifically detail more of the particular events occurring at the time of the history of the events detailed in the Holy Royal Arch. Consequently a more rounded knowledge of those events has been experienced and retained that give a greater understanding of the Holy Royal Arch that I hope to bring in presenting my explanations of aspects of the ceremonies conducted in the Chapter.

Read and Enjoy.

Ray Hudson
June 2015.

CHAPTER 1

THE BEGINNING

The Order of the Holy Royal Arch used to be deemed as the completion of the third degree of the Craft, as it is written and acclaimed in the UGLE Book of Constitution that "Pure and Ancient Freemasonry consists of only 3 Degrees, that of Entered Apprentice, Fellowcraft, Master Mason, including that of The Holy Royal Arch". This well used phrase is often used to make the other Side Orders seem superfluous to Craft Freemasonry, but like a lot of things in Freemasonry it is misunderstood and used out of context.

This phrase simply illustrates an agreed aspect which arose at the coming together of the Ancient Grand Lodge and the Moderns Grand Lodge in 1813-1815. It seems that the "Moderns" deemed their Masonic ritual to be PURE, and the Ancients deemed their Masonic ritual to be, of course, ANCIENT. So when the two came together that phrase, quite rightly, defined their ceremonies. They could just have easily have said *"UGLE Freemasonry consists of only 3 degrees......etc."*, of which it still does today. Unfortunately many current Freemasons use this phrase to prove their personal belief that all the other Masonic Orders have no value or merit outside of the Craft and Holy Royal Arch. How utterly wrong can some individuals be. In recent years our Grand Master has openly acknowledged the connectivity of all the Freemasonic Orders, and that acknowledgement contains so much sense as many of the other orders contain much more information that throws greater light on the Craft and the Holy Royal Arch.

I mentioned in my previous book that the majority of Masonic ritual is based upon Jewish history, religion and culture, and to fully appreciate the deeper meanings of the Masonic ceremonies one should understand the basis of Hebrew culture, their adherence to their religious beliefs, which also governed their political aspirations, their devotion to their family structure and domestic life, plus their spiritual and mystical teachings. The latter being obtained from a study of the Old Testament plus a book known and appreciated as the second Jewish bible, namely, The Qabbalah. This second book, the Qabbalah, teaches of the significance of numbers, colours and even letters, and so much more, therefore an understanding of these aspects yields greater profit in understanding Hebrew history which will result in a better appreciation of the Solomonic ceremonies, especially the Holy Royal Arch. Also, and it must be stressed, that any extra non-masonic research given to the specific incidents of which any Masonic ceremonies depict will prove of immense value and add greatly to your understanding of that ceremony. There is so much available outside of Masonic teaching that to detail it in this book would take a decade to prepare, but the wonderful web is a veritable treasure trove if you are cautiously selective. So just for this book and to obtain a better understanding of Jewish history, culture and religion we must give a careful look and appreciation of the details that give rise to the Order of The Holy Royal Arch.

Within Freemasonic ceremonies it is generally acknowledged that our Great and Illustrious founder was MOSES.

CHAPTER 2

"OUR GREAT AND ILLUSTRIOUS FOUNDER – MOSES"

That great leader who commanded the Exodus, built the first Tabernacle, and created the Israelitish nation renowned and therefore a much more in depth look at his life, and the events that surrounded it, should yield a greater appreciation of the masonic use of this enigmatic character and the instrumental events of the formation of the Israelite nation. To this end I made a study of the biblical life of Moses and formulated it into what I felt was a more logical and unromantic appreciation of this great leader, regarded within Freemasonry as *"Our great and illustrious Founder"*.

It has been, for many years, a keen personal ambition which has gradually increased in strength, to research, investigate and write about my findings and interpretations on the existence, life and writings of Moses, who is acclaimed as the author of the first five books of the Old Testament, known as The Pentateuch or Torah. Also acclaimed as the founder of the Israelitish nation, and creator of the Judaic faith, and by this derivative can also be claimed to be the indirect founder of Christianity and Islam, as both these faiths sprung from Judaism and therefore, in essence, all three hold the same God-head or Deity. To be perhaps the instigator of the three most powerful religions in the world, must demand some diligent research. To be aware of the closeness but vast differences of these dominant faiths, that leads the fundamentalists in each to extreme actions in order to sustain or prove their superiority over the other two, must merit careful investigation and consideration. Caution must be steadfastly exercised in order not to offend any followers of the three dominant faiths, but this caution must not be of such a nature that it detracts from the truth, or even the possibility of the truth. Bearing these important facts in mind I decided to attempt this tremendously difficult quest.

Modern Judaism, having developed from the monotheistic faith created by Moses on instructions from God, is an excellent testimony to the strength, importance and value that it places on the family, and this fact must be acknowledged, but at the same time we cannot close our minds to the fact that its Creator, Moses, according to Numbers 31:15-18, called for the massacre of boys and the enslavement of female children to Israelite veterans of the Midian War (*"kill every male among the little ones, and kill every woman that hath known man by lying with him. But all the little girls among the women, that have not known a man by lying with him, keep alive for yourselves"*). It is important to note, however, that such ethical dilemmas can be cited without an adequate understanding of the historical context.

So before investigating Moses and the events of his life,

we must fully apprise ourselves of the social and religious atmosphere prevailing in those ancient times, as it is those atmospheres that have the most profound effect on the thoughts and actions of the leading characters. Even today we are all products of the stimuli of our infant and formative years, the actions and decisions of our adult years being based on the acquisition of knowledge and experiences of those formative years. This of course would be no different when applied to individuals throughout history, no matter how far back we may go as researchers. The evolution of mankind appears to have reached its final stage, and seems to have arrived at its zenith of development. We have lost our tail, and acquired sufficient toes and fingers for all possible uses. All our physical attributes have evolved, it seems, to the perfection that we enjoy today, and have been so for many, many thousands of years. This would include our brain and thought processes. All that is required to improve their strength, resilience, and capabilities is regular training and practice etc. A reasonable pianist can readily become an accomplished musician if he practices regularly, acquires a wider knowledge from those greater than himself, and uses that knowledge in conjunction with his practice. This simple example applies, in varying degrees, to most things in life. As far as the mind, spirit and soul are concerned these function and improve in much the same way as the physical aspects of our make-up. The greater acquisition and understanding of the more abstract aspects of life, the deeper thought and reflection about them, will bring a greater understanding of all aspects of life, mental and physical and will put one in a much stronger position to be able to teach, guide and advise others. The higher levels of the Far Eastern Martial Arts prove to be a prime example of this theory being realised in practical terms.

History does prove that certain individuals who studied the mental and spiritual aspects to the fullest degree are noted as our greatest thinkers and philosophers, namely Pythagoras, Plato and many of the great thinkers of millennia past, Leonardo da Vinci, who managed to express his thoughts in his art and inventions, and more up to date, Isaac Newton, Christopher Wren and the rest of the founders of the Invisible Society, which was to become the Royal Society of today. Our own time gives us people like Sigmund Freud, Carl Jung and many more.

Those who accented on the physical aspects became great warriors and leaders, of which the annals of history records generously of their exploits. Those rare specimens of humankind who managed to accent various combinations of both these attributes, the spiritual and physical, acquired the designation of "Greatness". Prime examples are Cyrus the Great, Alexander the Great and Constantine the Great. Whether they used their greater physical capabilities to further promote their spiritual ambitions, or whether they used their stronger spiritual desires and beliefs to promote their physical goals is worthy of further research, but their calculated use of all their skills is obvious and indeed worthy of greatness. It is my belief that Moses himself deserves of this accolade, which I hope my writings will finally endorse.

Having briefly established the condition of humankind and its physical and emotional capabilities and limitations, it is of equal importance that we firmly establish the social and religious atmosphere prevailing at the time of Moses, so that we can more fully appreciate the use of these physical and mental attributes, and although the results may seem completely alien to our modern way of living and thinking, they, the results, would appear perfectly in keeping with all aspects of life in those times. It is of the utmost importance not to apply our modern thought processes and moral judgement on events that occurred in millennia past. What may appear totally wrong or dreadfully immoral to our modern way of thinking would have been perhaps perfectly normal and natural in times past, and quite possibly vice versa.

CHAPTER THREE

EGYPT AT THE TIME OF MOSES

The prolific number of Hebrews that were said to be living in Egypt at this time seems incredible, but according to Rabbi Ken Spiro, the 70 individuals that arrived in Egypt at the time of Joseph, had grown to a nation of about 3 million. This is not as far-fetched as it may at first appear. If each family emulated Jacob, and went forth and multiplied, that is had twelve children, you can easily compute that in five generations there will be this many people, if not more. This seems incredible, but is distinctly possible and credible as ultra-orthodox Jewish families in Israel today follow a similar trend.

This apparent "rabbit-like" multiplication of the Hebrews made the Egyptians nervous – "there are too many of them, what if they rise up against us" – and the Pharaoh issues a genocidal decree: "Kill all the Jewish boys".

There are many diverse and intelligent academic papers on who was actually the Pharaoh at the time of Moses' birth. It is my own view, and, it appears the opinion of the majority, that it was actually Rameses II. What all the academics do agree on is that the word of the Pharaoh was final. It is well recorded that Pharaohs were regarded, and indeed regarded themselves as "next to God". Their will was irrefutable; their word was obeyed to the letter. They were extremely protective of their dynasty and pure bloodline, to the point of marrying their sisters, half-sisters, or even on occasion their mothers. The only people who could perhaps "advise" them on occasion were their Priests. And this priestly "dynasty" also protected their own position of wealth and power by passing their positions on to members of their family by birth. Such were the positions of wealth and power of the Pharaoh that there were constant assassination plots, attempted coups, forced marriages etc. etc. So the actions of some Pharaohs in the "disappearance" of certain eligible members of their family, by means of poisoning, murder, exile were very common. Therefore to remain in power and control one needed to be singular, resolute and determined, and to entertain only those thoughts that prolonged your own dynasty. Any relaxation in these necessary thoughts would have proved a weakness, and this chink in your armour would have exposed you to the ready aggression of the greed of others waiting and watching closely in the wings. Under these circumstances it is totally unlikely that any "foreigner", no matter how well regarded they may become, would be allowed to get "close" to the Pharaoh or his "house". But then I suppose that one must acknowledge Joseph to be the exception to the rule, that is if the Biblical account of his life is accepted as being true.

Women, generally, were also held very low in the list of importance in Egyptian life. They were not given any formal education, were not considered worthy of conversation of any real substance, and fit only for reproduction, toil and physical pleasures. And to a certain extent we experience a similar regard towards females in the Arab world today. So it is also totally unlikely that any Pharaoh would have tolerated his daughter, even though a princess, to cock-a-snoop at his angered demand that all male children born to the Hebrew slaves should be drowned in the river. For her to blandly state that she had saved a son of a Hebrew slave from the river and was going to bring him up as an Egyptian Prince, and give him the name Moses, which is the suffix of the Pharaoh's name Rameses, which means Son of, would have been the ultimate insult, and a veritable signing of her own death warrant. This scenario beggars belief given the prevailing atmosphere of the time. Again quoting Rabbi Ken Spiro *"The only modern equivalent would be of some fellow who is meant to overthrow Nazi Germany was raised as Adolf Hitler's adopted grandson......You realise what a wild story this is if you imagine it in a modern context."* This is obviously an obfuscation for something else, or, as is constantly found, a metaphor for another actuality.

The story-cum-legend-cum-myth of a "leader" coming from the water, across the water, is a constantly recurring theme in many "creation" stories and prevails in most cultures from the Far East to the Far West, from the Ancient Chinese to the Mayan Indians of Middle America. Similarly, as the crossing of a bridge, or of water by boat, is used as a metaphor for the journey from life via death to the life hereafter. It is not difficult for an emerging culture to "borrow" this origin theme when the reality does not settle comfortably with their aspirations.

In the case of Moses, what could it be that perhaps did not sit comfortably with their aspirations? Could it be that Moses was not Jewish, and was, in reality an Egyptian? This possibility needs investigation, and explanation. It has often been found that "blind faith" or the total universal acceptance of a written story does not necessarily hold that it is actual truth. The Bible, that is, both the Old and New Testaments cannot hold themselves up for change or alteration in the light of newly found artefacts, scrolls, or the re-assessed conclusions of archaeology, a rapidly developing more precise science with the aid of new technology. The Bible, although changed and edited by up to possibly eleven times during the course of its earlier career, by varying factors of the different churches and governing religious bodies, remains very much a part of Church Dogma, and that very word Dogma, which is the root of the word Dogmatic which is applied in modernity to mean rigid and unchanging, perhaps despite recent confirming evidence, is why we have to ignore Church teachings as they would prejudice genuine research, we must therefore, turn our investigations to other contemporary chroniclers such as Josephus, Manetho, Philo, Polyhistor, Tacitus et al. Also we must consult the Bible, Koran, Mishnah, and Talmud. This way we should derive many overall views from which we should arrive at a more logical conclusion that more befits the culture, both Hebrew and Egyptian of those times.

This hiding, or for that matter, revealing of ethnic origins is nothing new and has been utilised, one way or the other since man has travelled or migrated. The American Negro is a prime example of this very fact. For decades they struggled for equal rights as American citizens, and finally and rightfully achieving their aims after great struggles and privations. But the majority, rather than referring to themselves as American, now refer to themselves as Afro-American, the prefix demonstrating their true origin and roots, and naturally commanding pride of place in their self-description. This also applies to Afro-Caribbean's, Eurasians, and even Anglo-Americans etc. etc. The Jews themselves further detail their roots within their own culture, such as Hasmonean, Sephardic, Levites and Cohens etc. etc.

Even if someone conceals their roots and origins, it would not take an expert long, after listening to the way he speaks, constructs his speech, and the general bias of his writings, to make a well educated guess as to his true origins. This has been done with great success on many occasions. To give but a couple of examples:

From the Sermon on the Mount, given so eloquently

by Jesus, one can determine, by comparison with certain writings from the Dead Sea Scrolls, that He was either a devout follower of Essenic thought and practice, or possibly a Teacher of this belief system to the Essenes. When one realises that in the Koran Jesus is known as Essa, and that Josephus designates the Essenes as followers of Essa, the conclusion that he was a Teacher is totally consistent with the times and contemporary writings outside of the natural bias of the New Testament.

Coming a little more up to date to Constantine the Great, the ratifier of Christian Dogma through his Council of Nicaea, we are taught of his vision, just prior to his successful battle at Milvian Bridge. The Vision, in the sky, was reputed to be of a cross and the initial letters I.H.S.V in Latin defining "In Hoc Signo Vinces", which meant "by this sign thou shalt conquer". Irrespective of the fact that at that time the logo of the Christians was a fish, the cross not being used until a couple of centuries later, and that Constantine did not actually speak Latin, his mother tongue being Greek, so it is most unlikely for him, or anyone else for that matter, to dream or have a vision in a language they do not understand. Now if one translates the Latin letters into the Greek equivalent, this is what you get, I.H.S.V. = J.E.S.U., together with the logical logo of a fish, suddenly, again, a different and more logical scenario appears. Revealing the lack of actual knowledge of the later ecclesiastic creators of this legend/myth, which to them would not have been a problem anyway because nobody else was similarly educated and able to refute their teachings. So the Church, by its structured teachings was able to control the populace and guide it in the way it wanted, or that the King/Pharaoh/Pope wanted. Lenin was correct: *"Religion is the opiate of the masses"*

From these two examples I trust that you can see and

understand how easy it is for legends to evolve and be perpetuated throughout generations.

CHAPTER FOUR

BIBLICAL REFERENCES TO EGYPT

Whoever is designated the authors of the Bible, which is primarily of the Hebrew culture and history, they, for some reason or other make continuous references to Egypt. It is accepted that it was the key nation in that part of the world, and would therefore attract a certain amount of attention, nonetheless the authors appear to have some sort of love-hate relationship with it. As Robert Feather in his "The Copper Scroll Decoded" eloquently states:

"All the major characters of the Bible, from Abraham and Sarah through to Jesus and Mary, had strong links to Egypt. Jacob, Joseph, Joseph's brothers – whom together with Jacobs sons form the founders of the twelve tribes of Israel, as well as Moses, Aaron and Miriam, Joshua, Jeremiah and Baruch, all lived for long periods in Egypt and were influenced by its culture and religions.

There are many occasions in the Bible when Egypt is portrayed as a place of safety and sanctuary – for Abraham, Jacob, Jesus etc. and it is also pictured as a place to flee from as in the case of Moses etc."

What are we to make of this quote from Isaiah 19:25?

"Whom the Lord of Hosts shall bless, saying, 'blessed be Egypt my people, and Assyria the work of my hand, and Israel my inheritance."

Is it saying –What was, what is, and what shall be? Is this the Hebrew Trinity signified by the Shin שׁ or as is always the case, the Bible writings are open to many interpretations, for those with eyes to see.

It is also true to say that any war is written up naturally differently by the winners and the losers, and the Egyptians are no different, all the aspects of their history that they could not control or change they obliterated, as the instances over Akhenaten, all others they chronicled as a victory. They did not report that they lost the Hebrews and their inevitable building skills etc. that helped a great deal in the building of the Egyptian Nation, but reported that they got rid of them.

Bearing in mind the possible Egyptian pedigree established so far for Moses', let us look at the beginnings of the Biblical story. Moses was born on the 7th day of Adar in the year 2368 from the Creation which was about circa 1400 BCE to Amram the Levite, and Yocheved or Jochebed a Levite's daughter, and who was also Amram's aunt. The only unusual thing about the birth of Moses is that his mother was supposedly 130 years old when she delivered him. She was apparently born when Jacob and his family were entering Egypt. Both parents' names have distinct Egyptian or at least Arabic roots. Moses' father called him Chaver, and his Grandfather called him Avigdor, but he is known throughout Biblical history as Moses, the name given to him by the Egyptian Princess who found him. He was apparently born into the company of his siblings, namely Aaron who was 3 years older than him, and an older sister 7 years his senior named Miriam, a name which has the distinctive connotation of the Egyptian name Meryom.

The first mention of Circumcision in the Torah occurs in Genesis 17:9-27, as part of the Covenant between God and Abraham. Each Hebrew boy had to be circumcised on the eighth day after his birth, and this is still the custom today.

Moses appears not to have been circumcised, and neither does his first born son Gershom, neither was Eliezer (*although very little is written, and therefore known, about him*) that is not until immediately after Moses' warning to Pharaoh that God will slay the first born sons of Egypt if he does not free the Hebrews, and the circumcision was effected so that Gershom would be "passed over" on that fateful day. This again being an indication of the Egyptian origins of Moses and therefore his sons, and in this case, particularly his first born. And although circumcision was a custom in Egypt it was not mandatory. So even at this early stage the biblical evidence appears to be building to support the theory that Moses was an Egyptian Prince. It is stated that Moses was uncircumcised for much of his life, therefore in Biblical terms he was not a Hebrew, and the Biblical writers would have wanted to have equated him with the Hebrews, rather than as an Egyptian. So they adapted the story accordingly.

Jochebed had managed to conceal the infant Moses for three months. When she could keep him hidden no longer, rather than deliver him to be killed she set him adrift on the Nile in a small craft of bulrushes coated in pitch. His sister Miriam watched as he floated towards the palace and observed the Princess draw him out of the water. Now I asked myself is this the behaviour of a caring mother. In her attempt to save him from being directly killed she set him floating towards the Pharaohs palace! A course of action that certainly intimates that she stupidly sent him to be killed! Why did she not flee with him, why did she not send him away with his elder brother and sister to her family of the Levites? No, for me, unlike Moses water basket this Biblical statement does not hold any water at all.

As I mentioned earlier the legends of origin from various cultures allude to a birth or arrival through/ on or in water. You can look at the legend of Thoth, the Egyptian God who created the world by the utterance of a single word from his voice as he moved across the waters of the deep. (Look at the Biblical quote: "In the beginning was the Word, and the Word was God............) You can look at the Mesopotamian legend of Sargon, dating back to 2,800 BCE and I quote:

"I am Sargon, the mighty king, king of Agade...my mother, the Vestal conceived me. Secretly she bore me. She laid me in a basket of sedge, closed the opening with pitch and lowered me into the river. The stream did not drown me, but carried me to Akki, the drawer of water...as his own son he brought me up...When I was a gardener Ishtar fell in love with me. I became King and for forty five years I ruled as King."

Change the names accordingly and you have the Biblical account, albeit in brief, of Moses.

As an Egyptian, Moses would have been aware of these older legends, but there is also a pure Egyptian legend much closer to home. The story of Horus relates that his mother Isis placed him in a reed boat and hid him in the Delta marshland to protect him from his uncle and enemy Seth. Moses or the author of the Biblical script did not have to look far for his "cover-up" legend.

There is also an Egyptian tradition that appears to have a great relevance to the story of Moses that most scholars seem to have missed. It is that tradition of well-to-do Egyptian mothers putting their children out for suckling to Hebrew mothers. Much the same as well-to-do mothers in England in older times did by employing a Nanny. Naturally this suckling procedure produced a bond and one can quite understand an affinity of a small baby and his big "sister". What I cannot understand is that, according to the Bible, this impoverished slave girl, Miriam, not only appears to have had unimpeded access to the Egyptian Princess, but had her immediately following her advice without question. One begins to feel, and strongly suspect, that the writers or reporters of these supposed events were so ashamed of the truth, in that the founder of their race, culture and religion was actually an Egyptian, that they became guilty of overkill in their efforts to disguise this terrible fact. A simple case of "Methinks he doth protest too much."

In those times the siblings of the suckling mother were referred to as brothers and sisters to the suckled infant. This fact now makes sense of Moses' protestation to God at the Burning Bush that the Hebrews would not understand him. Most scholars imply that he must have had some sort of speech impediment or terrible stutter, and therefore God instructed him to let his brother Aaron speak to them on his behalf. The only speech impediment Moses had was being Egyptian and being brought up as an Egyptian he only spoke Egyptian and perhaps a little Hebrew, sufficient for his adopted Jewish "suckling" family to comprehend but not enough for such an important quest. His "suckling" brother would speak for him. Aaron was of the Levite group, quite well educated, and destined to become a Priest, and quite an eminent one at that, so he would have been well versed in the Egyptian language.

Little is known about Moses's youth. The biblical narrative skips from his adoption by Pharaoh's daughter to his killing of an Egyptian taskmaster some 40 years later.

This timescale of 40 years, 40 days, 40 nights, etc. etc. occurs so many times in the Holy Scriptures that it cannot be taken as gospel, so to speak, but simply indicates a "long time" in terms of years or days. Although there are some peculiarly coincidental dates in Jewish history that I will relate later.

One traditional story tells that when he was a child, sitting on Pharaoh's knee, Moses took the crown off of Pharaoh's head and put it on himself. The court magicians took this as a bad sign and demanded that he be tested: they put a brazier full of gold and a brazier full of hot coals before him to see which he would take. If Moses took the gold, he would have to be killed. An angel guided Moses's hand to the coal, and he put it into his mouth, leaving him with a life-long speech impediment (Ex. 4:10). This story has no sense or logic whatever. If the coals were hot enough to burn his mouth then they would have seriously burnt his hand before he had a chance to put it into his mouth. This fable must be dismissed. If God had chosen and destined Moses to be his spokesperson and to lead his chosen people, would he have sent and angel to inflict or guide the infant to self-inflict permanent damage to cause a speech impediment. Only God alone has perfect knowledge and wisdom. It is His self-appointed definers, writers and interpreters that are subject to frailty and error. Again, it is my contention that the Biblical authors are guilty of overkill with this fabrication.

Of Moses' formative years, again little is actually known, but from our knowledge of contemporary writings and researches into the life of Egyptian Princes we can with a great deal of certainty construct what must have been his lifestyle. He would have received military training, and indeed we are appraised of Moses' military and fighting skills. Most importantly he would have been taught Egyptian history and all the rites and ceremonies of the Egyptian priesthood. He would have been steeped in the teachings and wisdom of the Egyptian pantheon of Gods, indeed much more than most as he was an important Egyptian Prince. The Bible confirms that Moses was taught "All the wisdom of Egypt", which must have been quite extensive. This teaching of all the Egyptian mysteries and knowledge would have occupied all his life up to the time of his fleeing. Among the many differing opinions that abide over Moses' upbringing and education, one detail seems to enjoy some consistency and that is that of being educated by priests. According to the various opinions these priests were either Egyptian or Midianite, the latter I disagree with, as I will point out later. Manetho, the Egyptian author, and High priest at Heliopolis, states that Moses performed a Priestly role in the Temple at Heliopolis. Heliopolis was known as the City of the Sun, and was referred to by the Egyptians as On. Manetho also quotes that Moses's original name was Osarsiph, and that he was named after Osiris, a very grand Egyptian God and a patron God of Heliopolis.

Today's monks and monastic clergy adopt a religious nomenclature perhaps following this ancient tradition.

I can only suppose that nothing specific is written in the Bible itself about this period of his life simply because it was specifically Egyptian, and would have given many extra clues as to his true pedigree and origin.

Of all the important aspects of Egyptian culture and religion he would have been taught, great emphasis would have been placed on the wisdom and teachings of Thoth the Egyptian God and Judge of the Dead. Thoth is credited with being the holder of all wisdom and knowledge and the author of many books, most particularly the "Book of the Dead", Thoth, according to Egyptian culture was the Creator of the world, which he brought into being by the sound of his voice. The astute reader will perceive the close similarity to the verse in the Bible, "In the beginning was the Word...............".

Furthermore Thoth wrote about a Flood, which he sent because of the sins of the people etc. etc. Thoth was also the Judge of the Soul when the applicant stood before him attempting to gain admission to the afterlife. The soul was placed upon one side of the scales with a feather on the other side. A set of negative replies to already understood questions was given by the applicant, some of which I list as an example:

No, I did not steal.
No, I did not forsake my God.
No, I did not commit fornication.
No, I did not covet my neighbour's ass.

And so it goes on. There are also other aspects in the Egyptian Book of the Dead, and other of Thoth's teachings, that were written at least 2,000 years before Moses, that one can readily see plagiarised or paraphrased in the first five books of the Old Testament or as they are also known collectively as "The Book of Moses". But then maybe it is pure coincidence.

If you are familiar with David Rohl's "*A Test of Time*", and the fact that this particular scholar and highly esteemed academic, has given positive evidence of a mis-placing in time with many of the Pharaohs, and that they are about 500 years or so out of sync, and when you place them in the correct time-frame, according to Rohl, you can then approach Ahmed Osman's theory about "Moses and Akhenaten" with a lot less scepticism. Osman's theory is that Moses was Akhenaten or at least his High Priest. And the fact that his, Akhenaten's that is, mummy is still not found leaves Osman to suggest that it is because he left Amarna with his followers, and that this leaving was the actual Exodus.

Ralph Ellis also proposes a similar theory in that it was Aaron who was Akhenaten, and his younger brother Moses was his High Priest.

CHAPTER FIVE

TWO CANDIDATES FOR CREATING MONOTHEISM

(was it written in the stars?)

One can readily see and appreciate the similar aspects of Monotheism or the worship of a single God, in both the creations of Akhenaten and Moses, and more especially the Solar or Planetary reverence contained and appreciated by both. Contrary to the majority of researchers understanding of Akhenaten's religious structure, it was not the actual Sun that was the center of his religion, but the Power behind the Sun, something very different from the popular modern understanding of Atenism.

There is not enough space or time here to digress into either of these two eminent scholar's theories, but suffice to recommend to the eager and enthusiastic researcher a thorough reading of both books.

While we are on the subject of the solar system and the understanding of the movement of the planets, it would be a good time to look at the understanding of these aspects within Egyptian culture at and before the time of Moses.

There are many books, films and T.V. programmes highlighting the cosmic and astrological qualities of life in Ancient Egypt. Many tombs contain the twelve signs of the Zodiac, lunar and solar images and references. The main God of the Egyptians was Ra the Sun God. The placing of the Pyramids alongside the Nile was meant to directly reflect the image in the night sky, The Nile representing the Milky Way and the pyramids, the then known planets. Hence the saying "As above, so below." It has been proved that the pyramids themselves, especially the Great Pyramid, are planetary observatories, designed for that purpose and much information is available on this subject. Naturally Moses would have been imbibed with all this knowledge and one can see the results of this acquired knowledge in the division of the Hebrew race into the twelve tribes of Israel, with each ensign, representing each tribe, emblazoned with the appropriate sign of the Zodiac. The four Armies representing the twelve tribes each had a banner emblazoned with a Lion, Man an Ox and an Eagle respectively, which were the representations of the four houses into which the twelve zodiacal divisions were split. And these last four icons were also to be found on the lids of the canopic jars of the Egyptian mummified dead which contained the important organs of their body, such as Liver, Lungs, Kidney and Stomach, and these icons were there to offer protection to the organs well-being and its ability to function when the soul returned to the mummified body. It is also appropriate to note at this time another incredible astrological coincidence, or was it?

I have always believed that astrology was yet another empty female pursuit, full of romantic nonsense, but I cannot deny my amazement at what I discovered some time ago.

The planets, or the astrological powers, of which there are twelve, each depicted by a particular sign such as Libra, Sagittarius etc., are again divided into four houses. These move through "AGES" which last about 2,500+ or so years. As the planets move through the heavenly skies the governing force, astrologically speaking, is the affecting agent on the various aspects of life. We all know about how the moon affects some people, and that it also has an effect on the menstrual cycle of many women, and,

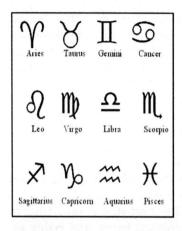

of course, the tides of the sea. With modern technology being more precise the scientists investigated whether the other planets had a similar effect on life on our planet. Sure enough, they concluded that they do. When certain planets, during their orbit moved to different positions the effect produced was measured to be slightly different, hence the sayings such as "with Venus rising" etc. with this knowledge we can now look at things astrological with different appreciation.

At about the time when Egypt was at its zenith in power, approximately 10,000 years ago, which was about the same time as the Minoan or Crete peak, the Bull was the creature and center of worship, and was for some time. The Egyptians had the Apis Bull and the Cretans were also great Bull worshippers, as any visitor to the Palace of Knossos on Crete can testify. This was known, and can also be determined by computer programmes designed to portray the skies and the position of the planets at any time in history or ancient history, to be the "Age of Taurus". Following this Age of about 2,500 m years was the

"Age of Aries" (the Ram). This was the time of the Hyksoss in Egypt or, as they are better known, "The Shepherd Kings". It was also the time of Abraham, and the fact that he sacrificed a sheep instead of his son Isaac. We have the stories of the Seven Horned Ram, The Paschal Lamb etc. etc. Then another 2,500 years or so comes the "Age of Pisces" or Fish, which was about the time of Jesus. And we have "Fishers of Men", the feeding of the five thousand with Fishes and loaves. We have the sign of the Fish as an emblem for those that followed Jesus. For those of you who enjoyed the famous show in the Sixties called "Hair" you will be aware that we are now in the "Age of Aquarius" or Water, and, as the news media is constantly reporting, we have Tsunamis, Floods, Torrential rains, and rising sea levels due to global warming. More water than we have ever experienced. Is this all just an uncanny coincidence, or is there actually something in it?

Another astrological phenomena which astounded me, and has a distinct Egyptian, Judaic and from these two naturally, a Mosaic context, and even a Middle American connection, was the symbolism behind the number 72.

Astrologically, because the Earth is not exactly a pure spherical orb and is more ovoid or egg-shaped in its formation, as it spins, it wobbles. This wobble causes it to lose a fraction of a degree each year. And it takes 72 years to lose a complete degree. Egyptians somehow knew this and incorporated this fact into their pyramids design and structure, as they did the circumference of the Earth *pro rata*. The Jews have the symbolism that it requires 72 Elders to form a Sanhedrim. Jacob's ladder had 72 rungs. There are 72 different Angels and 72 names for the Jewish God. As we learn in the Chapter ritual that the Jewish nation must not tarnish the name of God with the human voice or write it with the human hand because it is so sacred and precious, they have 72 substitute names or titles from which to choose depending on which context they wish to speak about.

In the case of the Mayan Indians of Middle America it is somewhat more obtuse but equally astounding.

The God of the Mayans is known as Quetzacoatl, and the origins are related that, once again, he came to their lands from across the water. He was fair-skinned, blue eyed and sported a flowing beard, something that was not within the Mayan Indian genetic make-up to achieve. He was obviously a foreigner. DNA and other advanced technological examination of Egyptian mummies have proven that they consumed cannabis, which was only indigenous to the South American Continent at that time. Therefore it must be assumed that travel between these two continents was achieved and that there was an exchange of knowledge, technology and goods. Hence the appearance of Quetzacoatl, the transfer of the knowledge of building in a pyramidal form and shape, and the export of cannabis from South America to Egypt.

In Egypt you can see the gradual evolvement of the pyramidal form from its early erroneous stages until its perfected conclusion, whereas in the Mayan culture the early forms and errors are not apparent, implying that the final knowledge was suddenly bequeathed. The point of this seemingly digressive aspect is to relate that many of the Mayan Temples had 72 steps leading up to the sacrificial altar. Is this another coincidence? A final amazing discovery of astrological connection between the Mayans and Judaic teaching is the story of Joshua who prayed fervently to the Almighty to continue the light of day until he had completed the overthrow of his enemies. The Lord responded, according to Biblical scripture, and the Sun stayed up for 20 hours on that day, affording

Joshua the success he prayed for. In Mayan culture there is a story that because of the wayward sins of the people, the Sun failed to rise one day, and research proves that it was about the same time as the Joshua incident on the other side of the world. Logically if the Sun stayed up for 20 hours on one side of the world then darkness would prevail on the other side, as is recorded in the respective cultures and legends of the two separate races. The scientific and astrological explanation for this phenomena is that a particular planet or comet on its approximately 26,280 year orbit, approaches so close to our Earth that the opposing force of its spin as it passes us causes our Earth to slow down on its axis, thereby permitting the Sun to stay in one part of the world and darkness to remain in the other. When the comet has passed us the Earth resumes its normal spin. Thereby re-establishing the status quo. The fact that the length of its orbit i.e. 26,280 years is again 72 times the number of days in a year, namely 365, must be yet another coincidence as there still remains a large debate on the reliability of certain calendars.

Or is it really another coincidence?

Did our ancients know something that has become lost on its journey to us? Is there something in this astrological rubbish? That again is something for another paper and a further separate investigation and discussion. What I have discussed here is sufficient for our present discussions and investigations. Next time you visit Grand Lodge at Great Queen Street look up into the four corners of the Grand Temple and there you will see the Astrological signs of the Zodiac. I have found that there is nothing within Freemasonry that does not have a definitive meaning. So why are these astrological signs so prominent within our Grand Temple? There is much of the old meaning of Masonic ritual that has become lost, and this loss does

not mean insignificance. We simply must keep on researching to discover the origins and true meanings of the
knowledge handed down to us.

We must now continue with our main subject for
research and discussion.....MOSES.

CHAPTER SIX

MOSES.....THE STORY CONTINUES

What better way could the Biblical writers devise for the fleeing of Moses than an affronted disgust at the treatment of one of the Hebrews by an Egyptian guard followed by a gallant retributional slaying of the cruel perpetrator. Already a murderer is being portrayed as a hero. For myself I like to interpret this incident in the life of Moses as a pure accident. That Moses had, in his constant education and religious upbringing, acquired a genuine respect for human life, a tolerance for different cultural and religious differences, and a very low tolerance for unfair cruelty of any kind. Although I have to accept my earlier observations of his apparent disregard for life as a systematic necessity of the results of those actions and of the times. Hence the defense of the Hebrew slave and the accidental slaying of the Egyptian perpetrator of the cruelty. Moses did not instantly flee after this incident but trusted in the confident silence of the victim he saved and that no-one witnessed the event, and burying the unfortunate victim in the sand, he went on his way. But after a short while, he was involved in a debate with two other Hebrew slaves who taunted him about his previous actions in defending their compatriot and his slaying of the Egyptian guard. Realising that his secret was no longer safe, Moses fled his native Egypt. But we must not forget that life was very cheap in those days and that the Pharaoh was totally all-powerful and his close associates would have held a similar power pro-rata to their rank.

Therefore a prince could have easily ordered someone's death without any questions being asked. With that sort of power why would a prince risk a personal murder charge, if it would ever be brought against him, and why would he deem it necessary to flee against such a charge supported only by a couple of immigrant slaves who were persecuted for any miniscule reason anyway. One would have thought that any reason that could be devised for getting rid of a couple of undesirables, in those times, would have been jumped at. One can perceive, I hope, that the whole story reeks of fabrication, when one looks more closely at the details and refrains from accepting at face value. I suppose that if this story was being written up or "created" some centuries after the supposed event when morals and values had perhaps changed, then the portrayal of a "prince" protecting a poor humble immigrant to the point of murder then it would add some hero type value to the portrayed main character, and therefore add some more credibility to his teachings and creations.

As I mentioned earlier, dedicated students of writing, its styles and format can discern whether a particular author is legitimate or not. It is not a finite science, but can prove fairly reliable. Even an enthusiastic amateur can see that the styles of the first five books of the Bible, those attributed to Moses and called the Torah, Pentateuch, or even Books of Moses, are varied enough to create sufficient doubt to the fact that a single authorship, even of Moses, is most unlikely. This is more or less confirmed by the varying names of where Moses fled to, and the different names applied to his future father-in-law, for example – Jethro, Reuel or Raguel and Hobab, who was an excommunicated priest.

It is ironic that the only consistency, among the writers

of this time, is of his having married Zipporah, whom the Bible describes as being black, and therefore became a member of a Priestly family and to have dwelt with the Midianites for a long time, and it is the one thing that sends my logical mind into overtime. There is much information available about the culture and customs of the Bedouin tribe of the Midianites that even the briefest of studies brings the Moses aspects to this tribe into question. They were a Bedouin tribe, nomadic, and most unlikely to possess a religious philosophy that would attract someone of Moses's background and high religious appreciation. Especially as their deity was Baal, an idolatrous God. For the past forty years Moses was brought up in the total luxury of the Egyptian high house, nothing was spared for his comfort. Is it likely that he would willingly serve as a shepherd for his father-in-law, when amongst the Bedouin tribes, and indeed as it still is today, it was/is the custom for the women to attend to such work. But an appreciation of the fact that the other great leaders of the Jewish people, such as Abraham, Isaac, Jacob and his twelve sons were all shepherds, so it can be said that the new leader of the Hebrews was following in his predecessors footsteps. How nice, and coincidental. Or is the term "Shepherd" simply a soubriquet for Leader, King, etc. Is the phrase "tending his flock" purely a metaphor for looking after his people? Again this part of the created story of our subject contains too many improbabilities and shows, once more, an over-kill by the writers to show great humility and reverence for their "hero". If this story is accepted how do we explain the passage in Numbers 31 which relates that Moses dealt such a cruel blow on the Midianites, killing every male including the 5 Kings and committed many other atrocities of vengeance against the Bedouin people.

There is, in the Midrash, which is the explanation

and commentary on the Old Testament scrolls, a passage which relates that Moses married a women from Kush, part of modern day Ethiopia, and the Bible, confusing as it might be, confirms this in Numbers 21:1."And Moses took a Kush woman for his wife." Josephus again in confirmation writes that Moses married Tharbis, daughter of the King of Ethiopia. The consensus of the writings of Josephus on this particular matter is that Moses was forced by the priests of Amun-Ra to flee to Kush. This is bringing us once again to the prognosis of Ahmed Osman on Akhenaten, or pretty close to it, in so far as that the displaced Amun priests were so irate at losing their wealth and power by the obliteration of Amun and the instigation of the worship of the Aten by Ahkenaten, that they "bumped off" Akhenaten thereby putting great fear into Moses for the safety of his life and that of his Aten followers, that they were all forced to take flight. And Kush, the farthest point of the Egyptian empire in Ethiopia was their destination. There was an official Egyptian office called "Prince of Kush" and in the light of the above, and in conjunction with the aforementioned writings of Manetho, it is not at all unreasonable to conclude that Moses did flee to the furthest part of the Egyptian Kingdom, to keep him out of the way, and to be given the title of "Prince of Kush" to keep him quiet. Whether this is true or not we shall possibly never know, but it does hold more logic and possibility than the dreams, wishes, and concoctions of the Bible Scribes in their efforts to apportion a heritage, culture, religion and history to their newly formed nation. Whether the reality lies in Midian or Kush, or even some other place, this must have been a time of great reflection for Moses. A time for him to dwell and consider and develop his views of monotheism, a single God, a single nation, a single cause, a single truth. We must now address the greatest turning point in his life, and therefore in the history of the Israelite nation, God's chosen children. The story of the Burning Bush.

THE BURNING BUSH

The story goes that Moses saw the representation of God, or his angel, as a burning bush, and heard his, God's that is, instructions. And it is stressed that the reason for this apparent miracle was that although the bush was aflame it was not consumed by those flames. This, I feel, is the greatest clue to understanding this story. The bush concerned and referred to is the Acacia bush, a fairly common bush in that part of the land around Mount Sinai, and not to be confused with the Acacia tree. We, in this country, know this bush as the Mimosa. To the locals it was not known as the Acacia or Mimosa, those are its western names, but it was known as "The Bush that

Burns" for this very simple reason. This particular species of the Acacia bush has bright orange flowers and when the desert sun shines down upon it, the shimmering heat creates the effect that it is aflame. Hence the apparent miracle that it was aflame but was not consumed. To the locals this was a fairly common scene, but to the Greek Scribes responsible for translating the Hebrew Scriptures some 350 years later, who would be unfamiliar with local knowledge and customs, it must have appeared to be a miracle, so it was interpreted and related that way.

Having been immersed in Egyptian Priestly traditions for the first forty years of his life, Moses must have been a deeply reflective man with a strong spiritual belief that would lead him to hours of deep meditation and thought during his many hours of loneliness as a shepherd whilst tending his father-in-law's sheep, if we accept this part of the story to be true. These reflective moments could easily have become so intense and profound that imaginings, mirages etc. etc. could have regularly been experienced. It is also wise to consider that Moses, obviously a deeply religious man, would have sought ways to express his religious feelings, and contemplated fresh ways of practicing his faith. Like most evangelical ministers he would have looked for new and original ways of understanding his God, or even finding a new God, a more powerful God than those that exist or existed before. Concentrating ones thoughts and energy to one objective has far more potency than spreading those attributes thinly among many. Therefore rather than spread thinly among many, which would therefore produce equally thin results, why not concentrate totally on a single deity that had all the qualities and beneficences of all the other deities put together. An all-powerful, all-knowing and ever-present God. The idea of a single God culture, which we call Monotheism, must have been forming in his mind. The desire for its formation and practice must have become so strong that at extreme moments of meditation that once possibility must have taken on a reality so strong that it motivated him into action.

Moses was in a world where nature itself was worshipped, but, it seems, like Akhenaten, who worshipped not necessarily the sun, but the power behind the sun, Moses chose to worship not nature itself but the power behind nature, the all creative, original and ultimate power. It seems most likely that when this powerful conclusion dawned upon him, that this was the time that God made himself known to Moses, when Moses was at his most spiritually receptive, God was at His most revealing.

When Moses encounters God at the burning bush, God instructed Moses to "Take off thy shoes, for the ground that thou walketh on is holy."

God identifies Himself repeatedly. See Exodus 3:6, 3:13, 3:15, and 3:16, 4:5, as the God of his forefathers – Abraham, Isaac and Jacob with whom He had made an ETERNAL covenant. There are many claims throughout the scriptures that God changed His mind, abandoned the Jews and made a new covenant, but this is not so, no matter how much the opponents of Judaism may wish it to be or see it that way. God had made an eternal covenant with the original patriarchs and He simply renews it at different times. At this point in Jewish history God has decided to instruct Moses to tell the Pharaoh "To let My people go", and it is important for all to bear in mind that it was the same God that put the Jews in Egypt in the first place. This instruction is in the first person, and therefore refers to the Hebrews as Gods people and not Moses' people. For the Pharaoh to have fully appreciated the significance of this instruction meant that he would have had to have known and understood the Hebrew God. This does not seem credible. It would appear that even less would the Hebrew know about the God of the Patriarchs, because Moses asks, "who shall I say sent me?". This is when God reveals himself and his name and the famous "I AM WHAT I AM" etc. Moses also admits his inability to communicate with the Hebrews, and Yahweh instructs him to take his elder brother Aaron with him to the King of Egypt. Moses protests his worthiness for such a monumental task, and it is what he holds in his hand is the clue as to why God chose him.

CHAPTER SEVEN

THE ROD OF AARON/MOSES

Throughout the ages the Serpent has always indicated wisdom. It started in the Garden of Eden with the Serpent in the Tree of Knowledge, and has been carried through the ages ever since. It now appears outside Doctors' surgeries, Pharmacies, Hospitals etc. The ancient Egyptians wore a decorative serpent around their head-dress as a headband indicating that they were the Wise One. In the days before writing, as for example pictograms or hieroglyphs, or even heraldry, animals have often been illustrated with their accepted attribute reflecting the attributes of the person they were portraying. If a knight, for example, was deemed to be brave, then a lion would be portrayed on his shield. If he was very brave, then a lion slightly up-raised would be shown, if extremely brave then the lion would be shown rampant. The classic example of this sort of portrayal would be the THREE LIONS first used in connection with Richard Plantagenet or as he was better known Richard the Lion-heart. If you wanted to portray a wise man then you would picture him holding a serpent, which in crude drawings might resemble a simple rod. To portray a priestly and wise man, then show him in priests' robes holding a serpent. This was how Aaron was portrayed, which was a simple but sensible portrayal. Now in the case of Moses it is not unreasonable to assume that he, as an Egyptian Prince, would have had a Royal Rod or Sceptre, with the uppermost part shaped in the form of the Ankh, which would have resembled a Crosier or Shepherds Crook. Royal rods are quite commonplace within the Egyptian Royal circle as portrayed on the many walls of the Egyptian tombs etc.

Now when Moses and Aaron present themselves to Pharaoh, he, naturally, demands some proof as to the authority of their request and instruction. Moses displays his Rod of Royal authority, and Aaron shows his wisdom by means of explanation. In short they both throw their cards on the table, so to speak, which is mirrored in the scriptures by the throwing of the rod on the floor and its turning into a serpent. Simply a romantic way of showing that their representation to the Pharaoh was wise and contained authority. The "advisors" of the Pharaoh then came forward with their reasons for non-compliance with the request. Illustrated in the Bible by the throwing down of their rods or displaying their wisdom. Aaron then steps forward with a much more powerful and wise argument that defeats the "advisors" protest. This is illustrated by Aaron's serpent devouring the "advisors" serpents. A romantic metaphor demonstrating that one mans wisdom

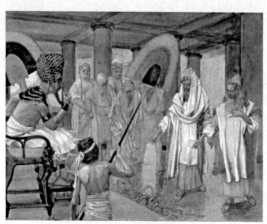

was superior to many others. The Pharaoh is so furious at such a loss of argument, that his heart becomes hardened to the request. Moses must now implement the Ten Plagues.

Magic in its old fashioned sense has been almost proved to be non-existent. It mostly resides only in fairy tales, legends and myths. The world would be a much poorer place without the possibility of magic. Most traditional stories would lose much of their potency without the possibility of magic. The worst thing about the modern technological world is its ability to almost disprove the possibility of magic, in its traditional sense.

Most of the "magic" or miracles portrayed in the scriptures can be proved to be non-magical, and hold a logical explanation, but in the hands of a knowledgeable expert these natural phenomena can become tools to procure a wanted or much needed response from the spectator. Just like an illusionist or modern day magician would procure from his/her audience.

We have all witnessed David Copperfield appear to make the Statue of Liberty disappear, or David Blaine perform levitation. In our modern minds we do not applaud the apparent miracles, but the cleverness of the "trick" and the expert manner it is put over to us.

Rabbi Ken Spiro relates in his Jewish History:

"Most miracles are natural phenomena with awesomely good timing."

The plagues, the splitting of the Red or Reed Sea, the pillars of cloud and fire, can now all be explained by one natural phenomenon. The explosion of the Volcano on the Greek island of Santorini.

This has been defined as possibly the most cataclysmic natural explosion/eruption ever occurring in the earth's development. Causing all manner of natural phenomena.

The whole cataclysmic event would put nature in temporary turmoil, and all sorts of events would occur at the most unusual times. That part of the world annually experienced over production of red silt that would produce a blood-like appearance to the Nile. Adam, the Bibles first man was produced from Red clay, his very name means "Red Man". The extremes of climate produced swarms of locusts, bringing varying diseases, lice, etc. etc. To experience an event that would throw these natural phenomena out of sync would obviously create awe and wonder in such an audience. And with a lack of our advantage of modern knowledge and understanding, would believe that it was either a gift from God, or a punishment, depending on which side of God you stood.

The incredible eruption on Santorini caused a pillar of smoke that rose so high that it could be seen many thousands of miles away. Indeed dust from the eruption has been found in the Nile delta and surrounding regions. In the daylight hours the smoke appeared as a pillar or cloud, and at night it glowed red with the intense heat. These aspects could well have been used by the Hebrews as some sort of navigational aid. The "cloud" covering the sun, could have produced adverse effects on the local flora and fauna, bringing plagues of locusts, frogs together with their usual dreadful accompaniments. The hail that was not frozen, but was on fire, would come from such an enormous volcano. Finally the falling into the sea of at least half of Santorini Island would have caused the mightiest Tsunami imaginable. This would have reached Egypt and could well have been the actual cause of the parting of the waters, as it is a factor of Tsunamis that they are preceded by a complete withdrawal of the immediate waters. The bigger the Tsunami the longer the duration of the water withdrawal. The vital point about this particular Scriptural story is WHY? Why the plagues, why the parting of the waters, why put the Hebrews, His chosen people, through all these terrible situations. If Yahweh was the All-powerful, All-present, and All-knowing God, why did he not make all the Egyptians drop dead, or even frozen them in time, so that the Hebrews, His chosen people, could just walk away. After all he actually created the world and all the living things in it, so the "freezing" of just one nation would have been a veritable piece of cake.

Again according to Rabbi Ken Spiro: "Judaism holds that nature does not act independently of God, and at the same time, God created the laws of nature and does not interfere with them. God is certainly capable of doing whatever He likes, but He doesn't play around with the physical world and its workings. Therefore, most miracles are natural phenomena with awesomely good timing."

OK then, accepted, but how did Moses know about these things, and how to utilise them to his and the Hebrews' advantage, and the total disadvantage of the powerful nation of Egypt with all its accredited wisdom and knowledge ? Once again, it seems to me that it is a very clever use of knowledge after the events and to weave them into a story that gives some history, religion and roots to an emerging nation.

There is, as always, another explanation. A few years ago two oceanographers documented, from their findings and evidence, that every 2,500 years or so the right combination of winds and tide will cause the ocean to split over the area of the Red Sea today. This is a lengthy process and is so related in the Bible where it says that the wind blew all night and in the morning there was a dry place to walk through. It is also independently reported that Napoleon, 200 or so years ago, witnessed a similar phenomenon.

You can just imagine the thousands of tourists now going to the Red Sea for their holidays and some deciding to go on a boat trip the following morning. They take an early night because of the howling winds. They wake up to find that the sea has parted and it is OK for them to walk through it. Would they declare "what a fine job the winds have done" or are they more likely to say "Oh my God, it's a miracle!" For me, I agree with Thomas L. Thompson and his "The Bible in History" or "How writers create a past." In that it is a clever weaving of known events by the later writers in giving this emerging nation some, history, heritage and roots.

Finally after the apparent death of the first-born Egyptians, the Pharaoh says "Go".

It is now left to you what you wish to accept or reject. In the meantime we will continue this intriguing journey into this enigmatic character and his apparent history.

CHAPTER EIGHT

THE EXODUS.

Perhaps the first thing that should be appreciated when researching such an immense event as the Exodus, is that there is no academically accepted archeological evidence whatsoever that relates to or can be allocated to this event. Such an event, involving so many people, even a tenth of the suggested biblical numbers would have left some trace. But no pottery, weapons or bones or any other evidence has ever been found, not even after so much archeological investigation has been made to find such evidence. Even though the Bible relates that *"they were condemned to wander harassed and embarrassed on all sides for forty years until all that generation save only Joshua and Caleb should have fallen in the wilderness"*, not a single bone, human or otherwise, in fact simply no evidence whatsoever has ever been found to support such an event as the Exodus. That many people wandering for 40 years in the desert, or any other place for that matter, surely would have left some evidence for future generations. The term used in the bible of 40 years should not be taken as literal. It is simply a way of saying "a very long time". If one goes back even earlier to Noah's flood, there again it rained for 40 days and nights, and then come forward to the time of Jesus and discover that he wandered in the wilderness for 40 days etc. One can see that this phrase is simply meant to infer a long time and is therefore not specific. Keeping ones faith in the scriptures aside this lack of any discovery of any archeological evidence would certainly indicate that no such Exodus ever took place, indeed many academics now support this view. But let us, for the moment, put this academic conclusion aside and try to examine this event as a distinct biblical possibility.

Throughout history much evidence has been discovered to support, in some way or another, many historical events, classic battles, ancient places and events such as natural catastrophes have been uncovered, analysed with the latest scientific knowledge and technology. Many biblical events, characters and situations have been confirmed in some measure in this way, the Great Flood being a prime example. Greater understanding of non-biblical contemporary writings have strengthened such findings. But nowhere, outside of the Old Testament, can there be found anything that relates to such an event as the Exodus. It is not recorded anywhere in Egyptian writings, and although we must accept that they rarely recorded their failings, none the less one might have expected to find something, a clue, a hint, somewhere, but nothing. Even contemporary chroniclers and historians record very little, even though the event appears to be of such massive importance, at least to the Jews. So it would seem that it never actually occurred in the manner in which it is biblically recorded, *like so many other biblical events illustrated earlier,* or that it was so insignificant that contemporary chroniclers and writers felt it not important enough to record. This has lead eminent scholars like Sigmund Freud, Thomas Thompson, Ahmed Osman et al, to re-assess this event and attempt to put a more logical explanation for it. So the conclusion must be that, either that it did not occur as biblically recorded, or that in reality it was so small as to not merit any importance. Nations and cultures that were, at that time, recording their history and development rarely recorded their failings. But one nations failing is another nation's success, so something would have been noted elsewhere. Perhaps that recorded writing is still yet to be discovered, who knows. But the greatest evidence as to its actuality is that there is no evidence, anywhere outside of the Old Testament. Now, as Thomas Thompson brilliantly states, if you are setting up a new nation, race or whatever, and you wish to give it some reason, purpose, root or culture or even history, then what better way than to create a story where you are all freed from slavery or persecution, and then find a place which you can then call your own, and with a personally prescribed history, religion and laws begin to create a nation that can eventually justify the title of "God's chosen people". The human psyche attaches so much importance to history, tradition and religion, that it would prove fruitless to try and develop a nation, or even a small kibbutz, without those qualifications. Indeed, even in our modern affluent and knowledgeable world of today, we can evidence the total power of these necessary qualifications. They can be described as nationalism, patriotism, faith, but in essence they are basically the same, something that the participants can call their very own, and it would appear that Moses realised the importance and power of these aspects and utilised them to the full. Later chroniclers and writers similarly recognised the importance of such values and perpetuated the created stories to maintain the original principles recognised and established by Moses.

Having established the logical possibility that the Exodus is yet another romantic biblical myth, what we should now do is make some similar logical deductions as to what possibly did happen by looking at other circumstances of that same time frame to see if the evidence fits better than the romantic one.

There are many academic speculations regarding Moses and the formation of the Jewish nation, but the one I favour is the one I have formulated from these aforesaid many wide researches and sources. It is my speculation or logical conclusion derived from the many facts contemporaneously recorded elsewhere, outside of the bible.

The key factor of this logical conclusion specifically revolves around the "Heretic Pharaoh" Ahkenaten, or Amenhotep IV, and it is to him that we must extend our researches.

CHAPTER NINE

AHKENATEN

Amenhotep IV was the most profound pharaoh to rule Egypt. He led Egypt in a direction that would tag him "The Heretic Pharaoh." He brought forth new ideas mainly in religion and art that would leave a lasting impression on the world. Unlike most pharaohs, Akhenaten presented himself in a way that would lead to controversy and would shock the world and his culture. Let us take an in-depth look at Akhenaten and discover for ourselves the man that would lead Ancient Egypt with much mayhem, not only during his reign but thereafter. To really understand Akhenaten, you must go back to Tuthmosis IV (*note the suffix of this name*), when the city of Thebes became the main habitat for Egypt. Its foremost god was Aten and was created during this time being set up by Amenhotep IV (Akhenaten) to be the main deity. Amenhotep IV eventually changed his name to Akhenaten. The new name took on the meaning "He who is of service to Aten."

Akhenaten's parents were Amenhotep III and Queen Tiy. His wife was Nefertiti who was probably a distant relative. The Couple had six daughters named Ankhesenpaaten, Neferneferuaten-tasharit, Neferneferure, Meketaten, Merytaten, and Sotepenre. Also present were two unknown members in Akhenaten's family. They are Smenkhkare (successor of Akhenaten) and Tutankhaten who was later renamed Tutankhamun, reputed to be the son of Ahkenaten and Nefertiti.

As a young child Akhenaten was raised in a traditional

Ancient Egyptian manner and observed religious rituals to the god Amon. In Thebes, Amon was the god that was elevated to the highest position. In time, Akhenaten turned his focus and beliefs to another deity called Aten. (Aten is the sun god or rather the power behind the sun and was taken into battle with Tuthmosis IV and later taken by Akhenaten).

Soon after becoming pharaoh of Egypt, Akhenaten discarded his royal name and loyalty to Amon. He turned away from old priests and began the cult of the sun disk -- the Aten. Akhenaten acknowledged that Aten was the single god, (*monotheism?*) the power behind the sun. He claimed he was the only person able to converse with his god. All communication to the Aten had to be directed through him, Ahkenaten. He banned the worship of Amon and closed down many other sacred temples. This put many priests out of work and caused them to lose power and authority and of course revenue. They were obviously extremely disgruntled, to say the least.

Akhenaten's wife's name Nefertiti was also changed to "Nefer Nefru Aten" meaning "Beautiful is the Beauty of Aten." The couple then moved out of Thebes to a new capitol called Akhetaton. Everyone from the old capitol moved to the newly constructed capitol including the court and artisans.

The new capitol Amarna was erected in 1353-1335 B.C. in honour of the god Aten. (Amarna is the modern name for the city called Akhetaten) It had more naturalistic styles and the art portrayed natural scenes and life-like figures. The couple raised many extraordinary buildings and conducted sophisticated ceremonies in the temples and palaces. His new capitol attacked the cults of other deities in Egypt, especially Amon. Sites of Amon were desecrated and any evidence of worship to this god destroyed.

AKHENATEN

Akhenaten even had his father's cartouches destroyed because it had Amon's name encrypted upon it. This continued to outrage the people of Egypt, most especially the out of work priests, and left the population uneasy and angry. Most of the cities in Egypt were deprived of their estates and plantations. Corruption fell upon the temples and soon they were dependent on the city of Akhetaten.

The art during the Amarna period had made a colossal and most noted change. People were portrayed more life-like. Unlike most pharaohs, Akhenaten portrayed himself less god like and more human. This new style of art was portraying people in everyday lifestyles and sometimes with minute details. Bek was Akhenaten's main artist during this period. The disfigured pharaoh showed an almost strange elongation of the head, large breasts, swollen stomach, and the diminutive splayed legs. He looked more feminine than masculine.

Not only did Akhenaten show his naturalness but also the surroundings around him. His commissioned paintings were detailed and unique in that they showed naturalism along the Nile River. The scenes of the time period showed the river engulfed with vegetation and wild animals.

Pharaohs in earlier periods showed themselves as being well proportioned and taller than their subjects. Akhenaten, on the other hand, was depicted as being at equal level with his surroundings that showed him in inappropriate scenes. Such scenes included him kissing his daughters and sitting with his wife in a family manner.

During the 12th year of his reign, Queen Tiy joined Akhenaten in his city. She brought with her a princess named Baketaten (Later Baketamon). Akhenaten soon provided her with housing and constructed a temple in honor of her. Nefertiti was no longer a favourite to Akhenaten and she soon disappears from the time period. Historians are puzzled as to why and where she left and there is much speculation as to what became of her. Her daughter soon took her place and held the duties her mother once did. This daughter was then replaced by Ankhesenpaaten. Ahkenaten soon found another queen who was named Kiya and might have been from the Mitanni heritage. At around the eighteenth year of his ruling Akhenaten disappears. It is strongly supposed, and there is sufficient logical evidence to support the theory that he was murdered by the irate priests. Much of the items referring to his reign were destroyed and demolished soon after his death. His mummy has never been found. At this time, and because of these events, many of the followers of the Aten cult left to pursue their beliefs elsewhere. (Could this be the event that was the inspiration for the much expanded and romantic story of the Exodus?)

His young son Tutankhaten succeeded him, and after a short while reverted back to the old style of many gods and re-instated the priests, probably from a heavy collective pressure from them. He even changed his name back to Tutankhamen. After a while it appears that he had second thoughts and attempted to revert back to the beliefs of his father, and as history records he was, like his father, murdered.

If you examine the events of Akhenaten's beliefs, his monotheistic ideals and read the Hymn to the Aten, supposedly written by Akhenaten, then look at the structure of the one god worship of Jehovah, created by Moses, and read some of the Psalms. Then examine the teaching that Moses received throughout his formative years, and look at the creation of the Ten Commandments and Law of Moses, I personally believe that there are too many similarities for them to be coincidences.

Knowing that the bible content has so often been edited over the millennia so much that it's true content has not come down to us, also being aware of more recent "un-edited" scrolls and writings that have been discovered and new technology that is constantly throwing new light on old themes, it is very difficult not to come to the logical conclusion that there is a solid connection between Ahkenaten and Moses. Sigmund Freud back in 1929 noted the distinct possibility and many other modern writers have made similar observations, some even concluding that they are one and the same.

I do not think that I would go that far, but feel sure that Moses and Aaron were somehow connected to the higher level of the Aten priesthood, and upon the assassination of Ahkenaten they fled the country in fear of their own lives and rebuilt the nation under one god elsewhere. To give the new nation some roots, heritage and culture many of the stories were changed and embellished accordingly.

This literal tampering is something that is not

uncommon, and under the circumstances can be understood and appreciated.

You can study the writings of Samuel 1 & 2, and you can perceive that he defends David's ferocious violence, which even for those times was quite horrific, extremely vigorously, so vigorously in fact that one begins to doubt the veracity of his writings, and it leads one to conclude that "methinks he doth protest too much". But then again when one is trying to justify one's choice for king of a nation, literary liberties are to be expected, and perhaps large pinches of salt need to be taken.

This, my hypothesis of the story of Moses, for me, makes more sense than the traditional recorded stories and takes nothing away from the power and greatness of Moses achievements, it simply questions the manner in which the greatness was achieved. One usually finds that much recorded episodes of greatness are in reality less romantic than the recorder records.

Having now detailed my hypothesis regarding our "Great and Illustrious Founder" and no doubt in some way or another Moses was great, but was he actually a Founder of Freemasonry, most certainly he was not. Almost certainly a Founder of the Israeli nation, so having established certain conclusions now let us continue with the investigation of the Chapter ritual and its messages.

CHAPTER TEN

THE HOLY ROYAL ARCH.

I regard it as an honour to share my knowledge and findings with you all, but I must again state from the outset, I make no claim of originality, I am not an Historian, neither am I Judge, but just an enthusiastic Masonic researcher who patiently sifts the wheat from the chaff, (and there is plenty of both), hopefully to effect a clearer understanding of this Supreme Degree, and to encourage as many of you as possible to commence or perhaps intensify your own Masonic researches.

This section of the book is on observations I have found during my researches, and in no way is it intended to diminish the supremacy of this H.R.A. degree, on the contrary, it is hoped that it will expand your knowledge and understanding, and perhaps give you a little cause for thought.

The sources of my research are too numerous to list as acknowledgements, but I am indebted to them all.

The main object of research is to promote thought and create interest, and to leave the personal interpretation intact. In every aspect of Freemasonry, the "*vehicle*" which carries the pertinent and basic moral message, is always open to personal interpretation, of which there are many examples by many other authoritative writers, but the moral message must always remain intact, and that is the most important thing to remember.

The first aspect that we must address is the title "HOLY ROYAL ARCH" or "HOLY ROYAL ARCH MASON". The word HOLY obviously refers to the religious aspect of the building and its reverential contents. ROYAL could refer to King Solomon, Prince Zerubbabel being of the royal line of David, or, as many Masonic historians prefer, to the King who patronised the Order at its beginnings.

The word Arch promotes many an argument, most believe it to refer to the "Catenarian Arch" mentioned in the ritual. Considering the duration of the ritual ceremony, and the very minute mention of the "Arch", I find this definition difficult to accept. I believe there is another explanation to this word, which for me, is more acceptable, and I believe, it is, or should be, directly linked to the last word "MASON". As I shall now explain.

If you take the word "ARCH" as a prefix, as in the words Archduke, Archangel, Archbishop and Architect, another meaning jumps out. In this context the word "ARCH" means "superior or master", as in superior duke, master bishop, superior angel.The suffix of the last word "Architect" comes from the word Tectonics, meaning the Art of Building, so we have Master of the Art of Building, precisely what is meant. I believe that, in this case, the word "ARCH" should be linked to the last word "MASON" by means of a hyphen, as I have seen it written many times in old manuscripts. This produces, without doubt, its true definition of superior or "MASTER MASON". If you consider the old rituals, whence this title originally derived, you find that only "PAST MASTERS" could be admitted to this supreme degree. In the Craft, of the same period, there was no degree of "Master Mason", only that of Entered Apprentice and Fellowcraft. As the degree of Master Mason did not exist there was no actual term Master Mason. Therefore, in the flowery vernacular of the olden times, the term "ARCH-MASON" would be the perfect way to describe a Past Master. This, I feel is confirmed by the symbols on a Past Masters apron, which are three "TAU" crosses, indicating that three steps had been completed, that of Entered Apprentice, Fellowcraft, and Installed Master. Put these three "TAU's" together and you get the "TRIPLE TAU", the geometric perfection of this supreme degree. The Tau has always symbolised perfection in some way, or freedom. Soldiers who returned from battle free from injury were distinguished in some way with the mark of the TAU. Slaves that were made free from bondage were similarly distinguished. In the Jewish Passover this simple sign was displayed on houses to encourage the Angel of Death to pass over this house. It is also the figure of the Cross of Calvary on which Jesus was crucified, and not the one as usually pictured with the extended upright. As I explained in my previous book on the Craft, the Knights Templar adopted this symbol and placed their feet in reverence to the Crucifixion of Jesus Christ in this position and it is from that action that we as Freemasons continue that tradition. The 3 Tau's on the Installed Masters apron symbolise that 3 steps have been completed, that of Entered Apprentice, Fellow Craft and InstalledMaster, and therefore eligibility to join the Holy Royal Arch had been achieved. Over the centuries the system has changed but the symbolism has not, and this does lead to confusion.

That this supreme degree was originally deemed the completion of your third degree, is open to discussion. If so, what was it deemed when there was no third degree? A completion of the Installed Masters Degree? I think not ! It must be that when they decided to expand the degrees of Craft Masonry, they added this modification, possibly as an attraction to encourage Master Masons to join the Chapter. If you intently study these two degrees, the Third in Craft and this Supreme Degree, you find that they are two very separate and distinct degrees. One is a degree of total loss, in that of the principal architect and therefore the secret of communicating the word. Then there is a 470 year gap. Then there is this degree of partial recovery, of the lost secrets and the method of communication.

There are some Masonic orders that cover this 470 year gap, and continue the story, between the death of the Master and the discovery of the secrets, illustrated by this Supreme Degree. Therefore, if you maintain that this degree is the completion of the Third Craft degree, then the Masonic degrees of Royal and Select Masters, otherwise known as the Cryptic Degrees, become obsolete and superfluous. But, Masonry is a progressive science, and these cryptic degrees are valid, and play a most important role in the masonic progression, as anyone who belongs to them will tell you.

If you look at the three degrees in Craft Masonry, they are, in their way, fairly similar in their construction and delivery. Then look at the H.R.A, and it is so different in its construction and delivery, not one officer has the same title as that of one in the craft. The whole set up is totally different, and it takes place 470 years later. In the three Craft Degrees the relative signs are preceded by the very important "step". This important part of the ritual is not required in this Supreme Degree, thereby indicating its unique difference, and highlighting its supreme importance to stand alone in this progressive science, and not to be a completion of a degree, which is in itself, although integral and extremely important in its own right, is slightly inferior to the H.R.A. Degree. Furthermore, in the Craft, as a Fellow-Craft, you are allowed to wear your regalia in an Entered Apprentice Lodge, as a Master Mason you are allowed to wear your regalia in a F.C. and E.A. Lodges, and so on. But you are

NOT allowed to wear your R. A. regalia in any Craft Lodge. Why not, if it was simply a completion of those degrees.?

To me, there is obviously a connection, but then there are between most of the degrees in Freemasonry, after all, it is a progressive science, but not enough to make it realistically a completion of the Third degree Craft ritual. For me they are very separate, one being a ritual of loss, the other being a ritual of discovery, two very distinct functions, and therefore two very different degrees. I hope I've given you all something to cogitate. Now, with the mood set, I hope, lets look at the main characters and officers that make up this wonderful Order.

CHAPTER 11

THE CAST

SCRIBE NEHEMIAH

He was born the son of Hachaliah, from the tribe of Judah.

He went to Jerusalem in 445 BC, to protect the welfare of the children of Israel and to help fortify the desolate city. With the assistance of EZRA he took a census of the people. He had the "LAW of MOSES" publicly read, celebrated the feast of the tabernacles, and kept the day of Atonement. He was an illustrious patriot, a judicious statesman, and a loyal, brave and generous man. Qualities all inherents of his title would be wise to emulate. He died in Persia and was buried there.

SCRIBE EZRA

The son of Seraiah, a man of great piety and learning who went to Jerusalem in 457 BC., to carry offerings for the service of the temple. Having re-established, together with Nehemiah, the "LAW of MOSES", he then returned to Babylon, where he remained for 13 years. After returning to Jerusalem he became actively engaged with Nehemiah in carrying out important works after the "RETURN". He is believed to have died in Babylon about 432 BC.

JOSHUA

Or more correctly JESHUA, was the son of Josedech or Jehozadak, born during the captivity at Babylon. he was the first High Priest after the return, a fellow worker with Ezra and Nehemiah. It is written of him that he discharged his all important duties with ability and faithfulness at a time of extreme difficulty, and in the face of many perils.

In those ancient times, this priestly role was as important as that of the King. As the Kingly line was kept in a strict dynastic manner, so was the Priestly line. They were called ZADOKS or Zadokites, and usually attached the term as a suffix to their names. The spellings vary somewhat, as there were no vowels in the Jewish language, but were inserted by translators, at a much later time, according to custom and tradition. Hence as examples, Josedech and Melchizedek.

The origin of this word Zadok or Zedek or Sedech is Egyptian which was, in that language Tsedeq. It should come as no real surprise that an important Jewish word has Egyptian origins as Moses and his followers have exactly the same origins. In ancient Hebrew this word meant rightousness. Interestingly in modern Hebrew, according to The Oxford dictionary of Modern Hebrew this word Zadok, or however it is spelt, now means CHARITY. Is it again a coincidence that a word that underpins the Hebrew faith, now means a word that underpins Freemasonry.

HAGGAI

Haggai was 10th in order of the minor prophets, and the 1st who prophesied after the return from the captivity. Nothing is known of his personal history, and so brief is his Prophecy, and so deficient in the poetic element and prophetic style and language, that it would seem to be rather the outline of the messages he was appointed to deliver than those messages in their complete form. The prophecy was delivered in 520 BC and it urged the rebuilding of the temple, and concludes with a Messianic prediction addressed to Zerubbabel as heir to the Messianic and Royal line of David. In this original context the word Messiah simply means "The Anointed One" a common term for a king or prospective king. It had no religious connotation whatever. That was to come much later.

ZERUBBABEL

This is not actually a name, but more a title as it translates as "Begotten in Babel".

His real name was Sheshbazaar. He was the son of of Shealtiel and Hadast, therefore a direct descendant from the Royal line of David. He also married Maukab who was the daughter of Ezra. From this union a daughter Rhesa was produced who married Zakhyath another son of Jehosedech. At the captivity in Babylon, being the representative of the ancient Royal line of David and therefore the "Prince of Judah", he was appointed by Cyrus, King of Persia, to head the volunteers who formed the first expedition to Judea.

BEZALEEL

As we are taught, he assisted Aholiab and Moses in the construction of the first Tabernacle, but what we are not told is that he was solely responsible for the construction of The Ark of the Covenant, in accordance with the strict instructions passed on by Moses. The Ark of the Covenant used to be prominent in the old ceremonies of the Holy Royal Arch. It no longer features under the ceremonies of Supreme Grand Chapter of England, but still holds prominence on the seal of the United Grand Lodge of England, in fact it is carved in stone at the top front of the headquarters in Great Queen Street.

THE ARMS OF UGLE · · · · · · · · · · · THE ARK OF THE COVENANT

NEBUCHADNEZZAR

King of the Chaldees or Babylon, who destroyed the Temple of Solomon, during the reign of Zedekiah in 588 BC, and took the Israelites into captivity.

This period of captivity lasted for 70 years, or three score years and ten, the length of time often mentioned in the bible as the expected life span of an individual. It is, therefore, reasonable to assume that all the leading characters of this period of biblical history, were actually born in captivity. If not, then they would have been too old to have performed their heavy responsible duties, with the dedication and energy that would have necessitated such an undertaking. All the traditions and tenets of their culture must have been retained and upheld, both socially and from a religious standpoint.. They must have been fairly free to pass them onto the next generation without too much interference. Indeed, it is recorded that not all of the Israelites returned from the Captivity, some remained, so the life that they had could not have been that severe. Babylon must have had a greater appeal for those that stayed than that of a "New Jerusalem".

BABYLON

Babylon is the modern word for Babel and actually means "confusion". This meaning is demonstrated in a modern context, but, once again, its origin is rarely appreciated. When somebody speaks in a confused manner they are said to "Babel or Babble"

JERUSALEM

In ancient Hebrew means "having attained peace". So you can say euphemistically, to leave Babylon and go to Jerusalem, that the Israelites left "confusion" and "found peace". The Masonic Ritual is rife with this type of euphemism, and is demonstrated further by the quote to "leave chaos and find order" or more usually "Order out of Chaos"

Many spiritually inclined Masonic observers define that the three sojourners, and their journey, represent the Physical, Mental and Spiritual sides of the human condition, leaving confusion and finding peace.Very nice and romantic, but I tend to leave the intangibles to those better qualified, and stay with the more tangible definitions of our ritual.

MOSES

This name, as well as the man himself, poses a great enigma for all researchers. We must look at this man once more and investigate his situation, as he is the one original intermediary through which the building of the tabernacles and temples started, and as these buildings are the "cornerstone" of our order, our researches cannot be skimped. And as he is referred to in the ritual as "The Original Grand Master", therefore of great importance.

The biblical story you are now all well familiar with having explained it earlier in this book. The placing in a basket and set into the water to be discovered by the princess. His upbringing in the Egyptian Royal household until he was forty. His fleeing. The burning bush. The Exodus. The 10 Commandments. The land of milk and honey, Canaan, which was to become Israel.

We must consider again that he was, for the most important years of his life, the first forty, brought up and educated totally in an Egyptian way, therefore his thoughts and attitudes must have been so governed. Bearing this in mind, lets look at his Name:- MOSES.

In Egyptian his name means "Protector" as demonstrated in many Pharaohs names i.e. Ra-meses (*Protector of Ra*) Ra being the Egyptian Sun-God and Tut-mosis (*Protector of Tut*). And he was a protector to his pharaoh, and later to his chosen people.

In Hebrew it is from two words "MOU" & "OUSHES" signifying "saved from the water", which, according to the bible, as an infant, and as an adult, if you include the parting of the Red Sea, he was. But, it seems a little strange to be named specifically for two events that had yet to occur. Also it is most unlikely that an Egyptian princess would give her "adopted" son a Jewish name. The Egyptians were already concerned about the expansion of the Jews amongst them, that to reveal one actually in their royal midst, with a Jewish name, would have surely tempted fate, and defied common sense. It would seem more logical that the Egyptian definition is the most applicable.

This study of words and names is quite fascinating and revealing, as I will now demonstrate. I thought of the three most distinctly Jewish words I could, and decided to check them out. I hope you agree with my selection. They are the words:- HEBREW, SYNAGOGUE & ISRAEL. One would think that you could not get any words more Jewish than these. Now let's look at them.

HEBREW is an Egyptian word, which in its original form was HABIRU meaning "desert prince".

SYNAGOGUE is from a Greek word meaning "meeting place"

ISRAEL is an amalgam of three Egyptian words, namely:

IS   from ISIS an Egyptian God
RA   from the Egyptian Sun God
EL   The Egyptian word for Lord.

So not all Jewishness is purely kosher!! I would ask you to bear this thought in mind as we continue.

When Moses was told to "Put of thy shoes...............", he was standing by the "Burning bush". Now this bush was the Acacia bush, as per my previous explanation, which was prominent in that area. Acacia is the Latin botanical name. To the locals of Sinai it was known as "The bush that burns" or the "Burning Bush", simply because it had bright orange flowers, and when the desert sun shone full blast on it, in the shimmering heat it did look as though it was aflame, but it was not consumed by the flames. When the Greek scribes were translating the Old Testament approx. 350 years later, I don't suppose they were familiar with this plant and its attributes, so they took it literally, and hence we have a supposed miracle.

Moses is attributed, by biblical scholars, with having written the first five books of the Old Testament. This is now generally accepted to be a fact. But were Moses' writings original. I will let you decide, by comparing the teachings of the ancient *Egyptian* God, THOTH., who, to the Egyptians, was the apparent first and most omnipotent God, dating back 4,000 years BC., whereas Moses books of the Old Testament date back only 2,000 years BC. Bear in mind my earlier statement that Moses was brought up and educated in Egyptian teaching and Mysteries for the first forty years of his life, so he would be well familiar with this revered God of the Egyptians, and his teachings. The story and teachings of THOTH are from the ancient Egyptian *Book of the Dead*, which is attributed to THOTH. You are all familiar with the relevant biblical quotations, so I will only quote those from the *Book of the Dead*.

Thoth was the universal demiurge who created the world through the sound of his voice alone, bringing it into being with the utterance of one single word of power. Lets compare this with the first words written by Moses.

"In the beginning was the word, and the word was with God, and the word was God"

Thoth was regarded by the Egyptians as a God who understood the mysteries of "all that is hidden under the heavenly vault," and that he inscribed the basics of his secret knowledge on thousands of scrolls and hid them about the earth intending them to be found by future generations, "but only by the worthy", who were to use the knowledge for the benefit of mankind. ....Sound Familiar???

He was also credited with being the inventor of all the sciences, specifically architecture, arithmetic, geometry, astronomy and surgery. He was revered to be endowed with nothing less than complete knowledge and wisdom.........Sound Familiar???

He was later taken and identified by the Greeks

with their own God Hermes, who, as you know, in some instances, is connected with earlier aspects of Freemasonry........Sound Familiar???

This pagan lunar God of the ancient Egyptians also resolves to send a flood to punish sinful humanity, and I quote:-

"They have fought fights, they have upheld strafes, they have done evil, they have created hostilities, they have made slaughter, they have caused trouble and oppression.....I am going to blot out everything I have made. This earth shall enter into the watery abyss by means of a raging flood, and will become even as it was in primeval time....."........Sound Familiar???

Finally, the last close parallel, that I will demonstrate, between Thoth and the God of Moses, is the Ten Commandments or Tables of the Sacred Law.

In the "Book of the Dead", attributed to Thoth, they are given in a series of negative confessions, that the soul of the deceased was obliged to make before Thoth in his capacity as divine judge and scribe. And I quote......

"Not have I despised God....."
"Not have I killed....."
"Not have I fornicated....."
"Not have I despoiled the things of God....."
"Not have I defiled the wife of a man....."
"Not have I cursed God....."
"Not have I borne false witness....."
Sound Familiar???

Personally, for me, these comparisons are too close to be entirely coincidental.

It is not possible that the bible passages influenced the "Book of the Dead" as the latter was written 2,000 years before the former. But the opposite is entirely probable,

Moses was, for the first forty years of his life, subjected to and influenced by the Egyptian way of life, and all its teachings and mysteries, so it is perfectly natural that his subsequent teachings and writings would reflect that previous learning. This demonstration in no way detracts from, or diminishes, the moral lessons in this part of the Old Testament. For me it is simply a transfer and an affirmation of the quality of the original. If, in the future, I discovered that the "genuine principles and tenets of the Craft" emanated from a source other than quoted, this could not devalue their merit and soundness, in any way. Sound principles and tenets will always stand on their own, no matter whence they take their rise.

The black and white chequered pavement that is constant within a Masonic Temple is called, among other things, the "MOSAIC PAVEMENT".

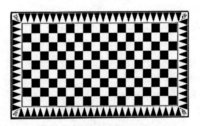

In accordance with biblical history, Moses erected the first Tabernacle, which was made from goat's skin and goat hair, and no stone masonry was used. He then went out into the desert and gathered up lots of stones and laid them on the floor of this Tabernacle to create a more reverential aspect to the building. From that event, any stones laid in a pattern are called Mosaic, which of course means "In the style of Moses", as Archaic means "In the style of the

Ancients" and Judaic means "In the style of the Jews".

I thoroughly detailed earlier circumstances regarding Moses, and I believe I have sufficiently made the point, so I will move on to other observations regarding the H.R.A.

CYRUS, King of Persia

A great king, warrior and wise man, who overthrew Babylon, and so started the restoration by encouraging the return of the children of Israel back to Judea. This would seem to have been effected by a direct spiritual appeal from the God of the Israelites to Cyrus. But I feel that there is one important historic fact that appears to have been omitted here, maybe to give greater strength to this spiritual appeal, for esoteric purposes, and that is, that Cyrus did actually marry Zerubbabels' sister, the Princess Meshar. Being a great king, like many great kings of times past, Cyrus was also a brilliant tactician and politician. By the capture of Babylon, Cyrus became Master of an Empire stretching from the Caspian to the Mediterranean and, with a view to the subsequent conquest of Egypt, decided that a friendly power, based in Jerusalem, would be a considerable strategic advantage. This object could be attained by repatriating the Jews who had been carried into captivity to Babylon under the previous regime, and securing their allegiance by marrying their leaders sister. So, I feel, that perhaps, Nepotism and politics were just as much agents as that of Spirituality in assisting the deliverance of the children of Israel from their captivity. Cyrus then set his wife's people free and appointed his new Brother-in-Law in charge of this deliverance. I can find no historical recording or scholarly opinion that the "Deliverance" was actually a condition of this dynastic marriage alliance. Although it must be appreciated that in those times, and for many centuries after, dynastic marriage alliances were always conditional in some form or other. History itself records that such marriages were even agreed at birth, and made for every other strategic reason, and the important one of love was never considered in the equation.

In the spring of 517 BC, the 70th year of the first deportation, a caravan of 42,000 Jews, men, women and children with their flocks and herds, together with the Temple treasures, (Ezra ii), set out for Jerusalem under the leadership of Zerubbabel, a prince of Judah, and Joshua the High Priest. Archeological evidence shows that the people moved along the banks of the Euphrates to the ancient town of Mari, thence across the desert to Damascus and south via the Sea of Galilee. The journey occupied 2 years and on arrival the repatriates found nothing but a dreary desert unoccupied except for the tents of nomadic tribes with their goats and camels.

Shelter there was none but it was decided that priority should be given to the building of the Temple, the people to make do with temporary shelters for the time being. Although Ezra is silent on the subject, it is reasonable to assume that one or more tabernacles were erected.

One tabernacle would serve as a treasury and storehouse, another would probably have been the Headquarters Offices, accommodating the Grand Sanhedrin, presided over by the 3 principles.

THE TWELVE LOST TRIBES OF ISRAEL!!!

This enigma had nagged at me for many years, even before I became a member of the H.R.A. I mean, how could they be lost, they did not know exactly where to go until the last moments of their forty years of wanderings. You can only be literally "Lost" if you have a specific destination, and in your attempts to get there, you go astray. It is my belief that they were "morally and religiously" lost and not physically in the destination sense. Moses could easily have taken them directly to Canaan, possibly in a matter of weeks or months, and said "Right this is your new land which we will call Israel, now get on with it". Instead he had them wandering about the desert for forty years. When you have ideas about building a new nation, this takes many decades of thought and planning. You have to get the former thoughts and religious ideals out of the way and clear the path for your new ones. This does not occur successfully overnight, not even in a few months. It takes decades, which it did, for Moses was not without his developing problems.

So they were not physically lost, and neither could they be of Israel, because it was not actually formed yet. So often are they referred to as the "Lost Children of Israel", but this is a misnomer. They were not actually looking for a specific place at that time of their wanderings, as there was nowhere actually called Israel. So they could not have been "Lost", and neither could they be "The children of Israel". It was not until they arrived and settled in Canaan, and called it Israel could they justly be termed the children of such.This appears to be just an appendage given centuries later, once again by the scribes or translators, who translated the bible many centuries after Israel was actually established.

The banners of the Chapter, the Lion, Ox, Man and Eagle are, once again, Egyptian in origin, and can be found in most hieroglyphic writing, which is not too surprising having established Moses' pedigree and background.

CHAPTER TWELVE

THE ENSIGNS OF THE TWELVE TRIBES
OF ISRAEL

PLUS THE FOUR BANNERS OF THE ARMY
OF ISRAEL

Having been invited many times to present my view of the Chapter Ensigns and Banners, it encouraged me to intensify my researches in this area, and to my surprise I found myself fascinated by the interconnections of these items with aspects that, at first, do not appear to have any connection with anything other than their original intent. The sources of my research are too numerous to list but due note and appreciation is made to E.Comp. David May, for which this chapter derives much information, and his researches on this subject. I am, as usual indebted to all my sources.

The Ensigns on the staves are borne by the Companions and are the distinctive bearings of the Twelve Tribes of Israel, and are figurative of a peculiar blessing bequeathed to each by the Patriarch Jacob, who shortly before his death, assembled his sons together for that purpose, as we find recorded in the 49th Chapter of the book of Genesis; the Tribes are further pointed out in the 2nd Chapter of the book of Numbers.

THE TWELVE TRIBES OF ISRAEL

NAME	MOTHER	NAME DEFINITION	ASTRO. SIGN	COLOUR	JACOB'S BLESSING & COMPARISONS
REUBEN	LEAH	SEEING	AQUARIUS	RED	AS WATER-UNSTABLE AND CANNOT EXCEL
SIMEON	LEAH	HEARING	PISCES	YELLOW	TWINNED WITH LEVI
LEVI	LEAH	JOINED	PISCES	DARK GREEN	TWINNED WITH SIMEON
JUDAH	LEAH	PRAISE	LEO	CRIMSON	AS A LION
ISSACHER	LEAH	WAGES	CANCER	SKY BLUE	COMPARED TO AN ASS
ZEBULUN	LEAH	DWELLING	CAPRICORN	PURPLE	COMPARED TO A FISHTAIL
DAN	BILAH	GOD IS JUDGE	SCORPIO	LIGHT GREEN	AS A SCORPION
NAPHTALI	BILAH	WRESTLING	VIRGO	BLUE	AS AGILE
GAD	ZILPAH	A TROOP COMES	ARIES	WHITE	A RAM, CHIEF OF THE ARMY
ASHER	ZILPAH	BLESSED	LIBRA	PURPLE	AS EVENMINDED
JOSEPH	RACHEL	ADD A SON	N/A	FLESH COLOURED	N/A
BENJAMIN	RACHEL	RIGHT HAND	SAGITTARIUS	DARK GREEN	AS A HUNTER/WOLF
MANASSEH	ASENATH	FORGET TOIL	GEMINI	FLESH COLOURED	TWOFOLD
EPHRAIM	ASENATH	FRUITFUL	TAURUS	FLESH COLOURED	AS AN OX

Joseph's wife, Asenath, was an Egyptian. Leah was Jacob's first wife, Rachel his second.   Bilah and Zilpah were handmaidens.

THE TWELVE TRIBES

Jacob had twelve sons who were named:

REUBEN, SIMEON, LEVI, JUDAH, ISSACHAR, ZEBULUN, DAN, NAPHTALI, GAD, ASHER, JOSEPH, BENJAMIN.

The more observant of you will immediately notice that two are missing from the ensigns displayed in the Chapter, and are namely LEVI and JOSEPH.

LEVI or the House of Levi was designated by God to be separate and distinct from the main body of the Israelites on the basis that they were the Priests and had special duties to perform and were therefore precluded from being the head of a tribe.

JOSEPH was Jacobs' favourite son with his fourth and favourite wife Rachel.

By Jewish tradition the first born son REUBEN would have been entitled to twice the inheritance than that of his siblings, but Reuben had been a naughty boy by sleeping with one of Jacobs' concubines, and Jacob wanted to register his displeasure. As Reuben was Jacobs' first-born, therefore by definition he could not be written off, Jacob devised a devious plan to hit Reuben where it hurt most, in his wallet!. This is how he achieved it.

Jacob adopted, as his own, the two sons of his favourite, Joseph, namely MANASSEH AND EPHRAIM, he therefore had 14 sons, and had, in one fail swoop diminished Reuben's share of the inheritance accordingly.

As Levi's, because of their Priestly role, were automatically out of the frame as a Tribal head, that left 13 remaining. JOSEPH then stepped down as he had 2 sons placed in the frame and was therefore quite content. Hence the remaining 12, as they are in the Chapter, were thus established, and Jacob's displeasure with Reuben was effected together with his pleasure to Joseph.

The ensigns are always, or should be, laid out in particular manner, along the South and North of the Chapter. This formation has no historical or biblical tradition whatsoever, but is done simply to assist the Masonic ceremonial and possibly to give a clear view from East to West. They were originally laid out 3 in the East, 3 in the South, 3 in the West and 3 in the North, with the Levites in the centre guarding the Tabernacle. There is a Masonic degree that actually creates this formation as part of their ceremony.

The Masonic Order of Royal and Select Masters comprises 4 degrees that detail the events of Jewish biblical Temple history from the time of the death of Hiram Abiff until the discovery by the 3 Sojourners of the Holy Royal Arch, a gap of 470 years.

The degree known as the Super-Excellent Master has the 12 Tribes set out in accordance with its ritual as follows:

"On the East side, towards the rising sun, shall they of the standard of the camp of Judah pitch with Issachar and Zebulun. On the South side, the standard of the camp of Reuben, with Simeon and Gad. On the West side, the standard of the camp of Ephraim with Benjamin and Manasseh. On the North side, the standard of the camp of Dan with Asher and Naphtali. Then the tabernacle of the congregation shall set forward with the camp of the Levites in the midst of the camp. (Numbers Chapter 10).

So the formation would be:

JUDAH, ISSACHAR, ZEBULUN

DAN		REUBEN
ASHER	TABERNACLE/LEVITES	SIMEON
NAPHTALI		GAD

EPHRAIM, BENJAMIN, MANASSEH

Which is a fairly standard format of protection.

EAST:

JUDAH

ISSACHAR

ZEBULUN

JUDAH and his three surviving sons went with Jacob into Egypt. We meet them again at the time of the Exodus, their numbers in the wilderness had increased to 74, 000 males. Caleb, the son of Jephunneh, represented the Tribe as one of its spies. Under Caleb, during the wars of conquest, they conquered that portion of the country, which was afterwards assigned to them as their inheritance. This was the only case in which any Tribe had its inheritance thus determined.

The Wilderness was a strip of sunken land next to the Dead Sea, averaging 10 miles in breadth. It was divided into "The Wilderness of Engedi", and "The Wilderness of Maon", a fact little appreciated and understood.

The banner of Judah was borne by NAHSHON, its Prince. It was designated by a LION couchant, surmounted by a Crown and Sceptre. Judah was the chief tribe, and was more eminently distinguished both for prosperity in war and peace, and for quietness at home. Its dignity was marked by the Divine Favour in choosing David from this Tribe to be the instrument of His blessing to the people of Israel.

To the tribe of Judah was assigned the most honourable station in the camp, that is, in the East, before the entrance of the Tabernacle, and under its Standard the Tribes of Issacher and Zebulun pitched their tents.

The colour of the Banner of Judah was crimson or scarlet.

ISSACHER means "hired", for Leah said, "God hath given me my hire".....and she called his name Issacher. He was Jacobs's ninth son and was born in Padanaram. He had four sons at the going down into Egypt. The Tribe contained 54,000 fighting men when the census was taken at Sinai.

After they entered the Promised Land, this Tribe was one of the six which stood on Gerizim during the ceremony of the blessing and cursing. The allotment of Issacher included the Plain of Esdraelon, (Jezereel), which was and still is the richest portion of Palestine.

The banner of Issacher was borne by the Standard Bearer of the Prince Nethaneel. It was sky blue, and was charged with a strong Ass couching beneath its burden.

The Ass is a patient animal and a proper symbol of labour.

"And accordingly, the posterity of Issacher sat down quietly upon the land allotted to them, and cultivated it with diligence and assiduity. Instead of employing themselves in war or mercantile pursuits, they were lovers of peace and quietness. The act of the Ass couching beneath its burden was an appropriate symbol of the indolent character of this Tribe, who would prefer a submission to every species of tyranny and oppression, rather than be at the trouble of asserting their natural rights in the field of battle. Like an Ass, which though a strong and hardy animal, would rather sink tamely under the heaviest load than shake it off by an exertion of its bodily powers.

ZEBULON means "place of honour". This Tribe numbered 57,400 at Sinai, and 60.500 before entering Canaan. It was one of the Tribes which did not drive out the Canaanites, but only made them tributary. It took little interest in public affairs, though responded heavily to the summons of Gideon and afterwards assisted in the enthroning of David at Hebron. Along with other Northern Tribes, Zebulon was carried away to captivity into the land of Assyria by Tiglath-Pileser, the Assyrian King.

Prince Eliab erected the Banner of Zebulon. It was purple and bore for its distinguishing characteristic a SHIP.

This was the Prophecy: "Zebulon shall dwell in the haven of the sea, and shall be a haven of ships; and his border shall be unto Zidon.

SOUTH:

REUBEN

SIMEON

GAD

At the Exodus the Tribe of REUBEN numbered 46.500 adult males aged twenty or upwards, and at the close of the wanderings in the wilderness numbered only 43,730. This Tribe united with Gad in asking permission to settle in the land of Gilead on the other side of the Jordan. The lot assigned to Reuben was the smallest of the lots given to the Trans-Jordanic Tribes. It embraced the original kingdom of Sihon. Reuben is "to the eastern Tribes what Simeon is to the western", Unstable as water, he vanishes away into a mere Arabian Tribe. In the great struggles of the nation, they never took part, preferring to idly rest among their flocks as if it were a time of peace.

The device on the Great Banner of the Division, which was borne by PRINCE ELIZUR, was another of the cherubic forms, a MAN, because Reuben was the first born of his father."The excellency of dignity and the excellency of power".

These epithets may refer in general to the prerogatives of the first born, which Reuben would certainly have enjoyed according to his just claim, if he had not forfeited it by his offence in laying with his father's concubine. And therefore his father predicted of him, "Unstable as water; thou shall not excel;" and then mentions the reason why.

"As water, by a natural propensity inherent in its substance, flows from its source in an elevated situation to a place that is lower than itself, so should Reuben fall from his birthright and subside into an inferior situation amongst the Tribes"

And the prophecy was remarkably verified, for nothing great or praiseworthy has been recorded respecting the posterity of Reuben. They were inferior in numbers to the other Tribes, and the pre-eminence was given to Judah.

The Tribe of SIMEON was "divided and scattered". They gradually dwindled in number, declining by about two thirds in the wilderness, and sank into a position of insignificance amongst the other Tribes. Moses pronounces no blessing on this tribe, and it passed by in silence. Like Reuben on the east of Jordan, this Tribe had little influence on the history of Israel.

PRINCE SHELUMIEL, as leader of the Tribe of Simeon bore a Yellow Banner emblazoned with a sword.

"Simeon and Levi were represented by instruments of war; the former by a sword and the latter by a dagger; in allusion to the abhorrence testified by the dying Patriarch, of the cruelty of these two sons, in the barbarous murder of the Schechemites, under the assurance of kindness and good faith".

Their father therefore said, "Cursed be their anger, for it was fierce; and their wrath, for it was cruel. I will divide them in Jacob, and scatter them in Israel"

Having been associated in wickedness, it was ordained by a superintending providence that their posterity should be disunited, that they might not be furnished with an opportunity of working evil upon their brethren, after the example of their progenitors.

Hence the tribe of Simeon had little or no possessions in the Promised Land, but dwelt in the midst of Judah; some of them wandered in search of a dwelling place as far as Mount Seir and the deserts of Gideon.

As for the tribe of Levi, it was entirely dispersed amongst the other Tribes and was devoted to the service of the Altar.

GAD means fortune or luck. Jacobs's seventh son by Zilpah, Leah's handmaid, and the brother of Asher. (You may sometimes hear it said to someone who has good fortune that he is the seventh son of a seventh son). The portion allotted to the Tribe was on the east side of Jordan taking in half of Gilead, a region of great beauty and fertility. The Tribe was fierce and warlike; they were "strong men of might, men of war for the battle that could handle shield and buckler, their faces the faces of lions, and rose upon the mountains for swiftness." Barzillai and Elijah were of this Tribe. It was carried into captivity at the same time as the other Tribes of the Northern kingdom, by the Assyrian King, Tiglath-Pileser.

PRINCE ELIASAPH was in charge of the Banner of GAD. It was white and was emblazoned with a troop of horsemen.

GAD signifies a troop; and it was in allusion to the name that Jacob foretold the difficulties that would oppose the progress of their posterity by the hostility of their neighbours.

But though they were doomed to be sometimes defeated, yet in the end, by divine assistance, they should overcome all difficulties and establish themselves firmly and peaceably in the portion allotted to them.

This prophecy was fulfilled to the letter; for the Tribe occupying a country beyond Jordan were necessarily exposed to the incursions of the Ammonites, from whom they suffered severely; but at length through the military talents of Jephthah, the Ammonites were finally subdued and troubled them no more.

WEST:

The Tribe of EPHRAIM took precedence over Manasseh by virtue of Jacob's blessing. The descendants of Joseph formed two of the Tribes of Israel, whereas each of the other sons of Jacob was a founder of only one Tribe. Thus there were, in reality, thirteen Tribes, but the number twelve was preserved by excluding that of Levi when Ephraim and Manasseh are mentioned separately. At the time of the Exodus they numbered 40,500 but on reaching the Promised Land, numbered only 32,500.

PRINCE ELISHAMA bore the green banner of the Tribe of Ephraim, which was consecrated with the figure of a cherubic emblem of the Deity that is an OX, which denoted patient industry and strength. His name means "whom God hears", and there are references to "A prince of Benjamin, grandfather of Joshua", "One of David's sons", and "a priest sent by Jehosaphat to teach the people the law."

Ephraim stepped into the inheritance of his father Joseph, and was elevated into one of the leading Tribes of Israel.

Thus Jehovah said, "Ephraim is the strength of mine head."

For more than 500 years, Ephraim with its two independent Tribes of Manasseh and Benjamin, exercised undisputed pre-eminence. Joshua the first conqueror, Gideon the greatest of the Judges, and Saul the first king, belonged to one or either of the three Tribes. Among the causes which operated to bring about the disruption of Israel was Ephraim's jealousy of the growing power of Judah. From the settlement of Canaan until the time of David and Solomon, Ephraim had held the place of honour among the Tribes. But when Jerusalem became the capital of the kingdom, and the centre of power and worship for the whole nation of Israel, Ephraim declined in influence.

The elder of the two sons of Joseph was MANASSEH. He and his brother Ephraim were afterwards adopted by Jacob as his own sons. Together with Ephraim they camped on the west side of the Tabernacle and according to the census at Sinai the Tribe then numbered 32,200. Forty years later, its numbers had increased to 52,700 and at this time was the most distinguished of all the Tribes.

PRINCE GAMALIEL led the Tribe of Manasseh. Their tents were pitched under a flesh-coloured banner, which was charged with luxuriant vine planted by the side of a wall, which its tendrils overhung. Joseph is a fruitful bough growing by a well-watered soil, and shooting forth two luxuriant branches. This referred to the Tribes of Ephraim and Manasseh, and the prediction was fulfilled by future pre-eminence.

Of Joseph it was said; "The archers sorely grieved him and shot at him, and hated him". Which referred to the persecutions of his brethren who sold him into Egypt, and to false accusations of which he was thrown into prison. "But his bow abode in strength, and the arms of his hands were made strong by the mighty God of Jacob. And his enemies were termed archers, so he is here said to be armed with the bow in his own defence, by which he triumphed over all his enemies, and rose to the highest state of worldly prosperity.

BENJAMIN was the younger son of Jacob by Rachel. His birth took place on the road between Bethel and Bethlehem, a short distance from the latter. His mother died from giving birth, and with her last breath named him Ben-oni, son of my pain, a name which was later changed by his father to Benjamin meaning "son of the south". The Tribe numbered 35,400 at the Exodus, the second smallest. At the entrance to Canaan, it counted 45,600 warriors. The history of the Tribe contains a sad record of desolating civil war in which they were engaged with the other eleven Tribes. As a result they were nearly decimated. The Tribe was particularly famous for its archers.

ABIDAN Prince of the Tribe of Benjamin, was designated by a Green Banner emblazoned with a wolf, because it was ever a warlike and cruel Tribe. It was predicted; "Benjamin shall raven as a wolf; in the morning he shall devour the prey, and at night he shall divide the spoil".

Though Benjamin was a favourite with Jacob, as being his youngest son, yet he conferred no particular blessing upon him, but describes him as a father of a fierce and warlike people. This is evident proof that Jacob acted under the influence of Divine inspiration. The Tribe accordingly partook of the character thus predicted. They made war singlehandedly against the other Tribes, and overcame them in battle. Saul, who sprang from this Tribe, also possessed great military talents. His whole life was spent in war, and at length, he, as well as his two sons, was slain in battle.

NORTH:

DAN was the fifth son of Jacob. His mother was Bilhah, Rachel's maid. The blessing pronounced on him by his father was "Dan shall judge his people.", probably an allusion to Samson, who was of the Tribe of Dan. The

Tribe was on the North side of the Tabernacle and was the last of the Tribes to receive a portion of the Land of Promise. The territory of Dan, though small, was very fertile. It included in it the cities of Lydda, Ekron and Joppa, which formed its northern boundary. Squeezed into the narrow strip between the mountains and the sea, they longed for a wider space. In time, 600 Danites girded on their weapons of war, and taking with them their wives and children, marched to the foot of Hermon, and fought against Leshem, and took it from the Sidonians, and dwelt therein, and changed the name of the conquered town to Dan. There remains, however, no record of any noble deed wrought by the degenerate Tribe. Their name disappears from the roll-book of the natural and the spiritual Israel.

PRINCE AHIEZER bore the Banner which was of a bright green colour, and charged with an Eagle, (*which originally was a Scorpion. The Eagle was anathema to the later Jews, it being the dominant symbol of Rome, their oppressors. When the Jews revolted against Rome, the first thing they did was to remove the carving of an Eagle from the doors of the Temple, which had been placed there by their oppressors. RWH.*), a component part of the Cherubim, denoting wisdom and sublimity.

The name Dan signifies "judging" as Jacob said, "Dan shall judge his people", or in other words that the Tribe should be the head of one of the greatest divisions in the wilderness.

He said further, "Dan shall be a serpent by the way", (*further symbolised by the scorpion*), and the Tribe of Dan was remarkable for defeating their enemies rather by policy than by force, of which there are many instances in the Bible. The Tribe of Dan, however, were ring-leaders of idolatry, and were the first who were apostatised from God.

ASHER means "happy". He was Jacob's eighth son; his mother was Zilpah, Leah's handmaid. Of the Tribe founded by him, nothing is recorded beyond its holding a place in the list of Tribes. It increased in numbers almost thirty percent during the wanderings in the wilderness. Asher and Simeon were the only tribes west of the Jordan which furnished no hero or judge for the nation. Anna, the prophetess and daughter of Phanuel, was of this Tribe.

PRINCE PAGIEL unfurled the banner of Asher, which bore a flourishing Tree or Cup. Its colour was Purple.

Asher's tribe is promised a tract in the Holy Land which should be fruitful and prolific, and accordingly it produced the necessities of life in abundance, and Mount Carmel abounded with the choicest fruits.

NAPHTALI The child's name is derived from the folk etymology meaning "my struggle" and reflects Rachel's rivalry with Leah for bearing children to Jacob (Gen 30:1-8).

At the Exodus this Tribe numbered 53,400 adult males, but at the close of the wanderings they numbered only 45,400. Along with Dan and Asher, they formed "the camp of Dan" under a common standard. The territory of Naphtali extended to about 800 square miles, being double that of Issachar. It comprehended a greater variety of rich and beautiful scenery and of soil and climate that fell to the lot of any other Tribe. The region around Kadesh, one of its towns, was originally called Galil, a name afterwards given to the whole northern division of Canaan. A large number of foreigners settled there among the mountains, and hence it was called "Galilee of the Gentiles". The southern portion has been called the "Garden of Palestine". In the reign of Pekah, king of Israel, the Assyrians under their king, Tiglath-Pileser, swept over the whole north of Israel and carried those people into captivity.

PRINCE AHIRA, a name that means brother of evil, or unlucky was the chief of the Tribe at the time of the Exodus and bore the banner which was designated by a Hind and its colour was blue.

"Naphtali" is a Hind let loose; "He giveth goodly words". This prophecy denotes that the posterity of Naphtali should be a spirited and free people; and that the Tribe should be fruitful and undergo a prodigious increase. And thus from four sons, which Naphtali brought with him into Egypt, proceeded upwards of 50,000 descendants when they were emancipated from their captivity.

Their portion was in upper Galilee, a country always noted for the productiveness of its soil. This agrees with the blessing given to the Tribes by Moses, "O Naphtali, satisfied with favour and full with the blessing of the Lord."

In his blessing of his sons, Jacob attached a description or definition of the names that he gave them Furthermore colours that relate to the breastplate or Ephod which was worn by the High Priest also relate to the 12 tribes together with a strict placing of the relative precious coloured stone designated to the particular tribe. The astrological signs that relate to each tribe and all the previous relative information, I have "charted" separately .

BANNER DESIGNS

REUBEN	RED	WAVY LINES-WATER
SIMEON & LEVI	YELLOW	A DAGGER
JUDAH	CRIMSON	A LION
DAN	GREEN	A SERPENT
NAPHTALI	BLUE	A HIND
GAD	WHITE	A TROOP OF HORSEMEN
ASHER	PURPLE,	A CUP

ISSACHER	SKY BLUE	AN ASS
ZEBULON	PURPLE,	A SHIP
BENJAMIN	DARK GREEN	A WOLF
MANASSEH	FLESH COLOUR	OXEN
EPHRAIM	FLESH COLOUR	OXEN

For those who wish to know the sequence in which the Ensigns are stood in the Chapter, here is the mnemonic:

From West to East on the South side. *Every Good Sailor Rubs Zambuca In*.

From West to East on the North side, *My Brother Dan 'As No Jam*.

As I have made reference to the astrological aspects of these ensigns, it is but right that I now show greater detail as to their relevance.

With regard to the subject of Astrology, like myself, I suspect that you also considered the subject some sort of feminine trivia. A subject left to the dreams and romances of the female of the species. Now, that is not the case, as science has officially recognised Astrology as a full science. This recognition does not refer to the possibility of "meeting a tall dark handsome stranger" or "winning the lottery", or any other of the more popular newspaper speculations. The recognition has been afforded after research into the effect that planets do have upon this earth and its residents. As the moon and the sun have a positive effect on this earth and its inhabitants it is now fully accepted that other planets, either independently or together in some form or other, have an effect in a like manner as that of the sun and moon.

Many Masonic Temples display the signs of the Zodiac, including the United Grand Lodge of England which holds them in prominence around the walls of the Grand

Temple. References are made to the Sun and the Moon and the Seven known planets, the latter adorning the ceilings of Temples. In my experience there is nothing in Freemasonry that does not have a meaning, significance or relevance. We must therefore look a little closer.

It is now accepted that the Egyptian Pyramids, for whatever the main reason was, were also built and used as planetary observatories. Archaeologists and historians now agree that sufficient evidence is now available to support this claim.

We know that Moses, one of our Grand Originals of the Chapter, spent the first 40 years of his life as an Egyptian Prince and would have been educated and exposed to all this knowledge. He being the progenitor of the Jewish faith and culture, we cannot be surprised that much of this learning is evident in the early formation of Israel, which was, of course, under his guidance.

It can be genuinely believed that his navigation through the desert to the land of milk and honey, was made by way of the stars, just like you would if navigating across the sea. The time factor quoted in the bible of 40 years, I believe, was not because they were lost but for the simple reason that Moses had to undo a multitude of factors regarding religion and culture with the older generation, then install his new ones and wait for the older generation to die, which made things a little easier to install his new ideas with the new generation. With his knowledge and faith in the movement and regularity of the stars in conjunction with the phases of the moon, one can perhaps now fully appreciate the importance placed on astrology in those far off times. Knowledge and understanding of this type would have been beyond the masses and known only to the priesthood, which in turn astounded the masses and led them to hold the priesthood in holy awe.

Numbers held special meanings to the Hebrews, and a full demonstration is not for this book, but one can readily see certain important factors relating to the number 12. The Zodiac, The months of the year, the Disciples, etc.etc.

The Zodiac, astrologically, is divided into 4 "houses". These houses are again represented astrologically by the Banners that represented the 4 armies of Israel. These are displayed in the Chapter and represent, A Man, A Lion, An Ox and an Eagle.

Originally the Eagle was not part of the banners, it was the Scorpion that first held that distinction. These banners as well as referring to astrological zodiacal signs also held attributes, these factors I have listed below.

MAN	LION	OX	EAGLE/SCORPION
AQUARIUS	LEO	TAURUS	SCORPIO
INTEGRITY	STRENGTH	PATIENCE	PROMPTNESS
UNDERSTANDING	POWER	ASSIDUITY	CELERITY

Whether it is accepted or not that Astrology is a science, it cannot be denied that the zodiacal references seen with the banners and ensigns is much, much more than a passing coincidence, and like many aspects of Masonic symbolism, hold much logic and serious meaning.

Is this all coincidence, or is there some substance of meaning being inferred from the ancient times to our time. We must remember that the written word is comparatively recent; there was little point in developing the written word if only a few could actually read. The important messages for the masses were displayed in picture and symbol form. This is why, in the earlier cultures so many statues and wall murals etc.etc were prominent. There would be no point in putting a plaque outside a temple denoting who it was dedicated to and who built it if nobody could read, but a statue or statues or symbolic pictographic representations carrying all the information for the reader makes perfect sense. If you take this system of relaying information to its romantic and artistic level you can plainly see the intricate levels that these "carriers" of information could be taken in informing the avid "reader". Because of the simplicity of the written word we have lost the talent of portraying information in this way, and consequently also lost the art of fully "reading", understanding and appreciating it

I hope in this brief chapter I have managed to bring you all something of interest, something that assists in your understanding of our beautiful Chapter ritual, and something that perhaps may encourage you into a bit of research for yourselves.

CHAPTER THIRTEEN

JEHOVAH

Now we come to that most enigmatic of names, the unmentionable and ineffable name of T.T.A.L.G.M.H, the sole name on which the H.R.A. Ritual pivots.

This name and designation is so fascinating that it merits a complete lecture to itself. JEHOVAH is a modern interpretation of the name YAHWEH, or as it was originally written by the Jews, as they had no vowels, YHWH.

It means "Bringer of Children". This fits conveniently, for lots of theological scholars, who advocate the old story that Yahweh sired Adam and Eve through the Primus Matriarch known as Lilith, in old legend. That this name or title Jehovah refers back to Adam has some basis as I will explain.

The Jews, who were continuously, throughout their history, a persecuted race, as the Exodus, Captivity, and later the Occupation by the Romans, and later testimony confirms, by Universal condemnation culminating in the Holocaust, amply illustrates. How they regard themselves as "Gods Chosen People" I will never understand. If this is what "Chosen" means, I think I will stay unselected!!

They constantly hid their traditions and beliefs from the "eyes of the profane".Disguising them for those "with eyes to see". They were also very fastidious in humbling themselves before their God, not only physically but metaphorically in a literal sense. Many of their most revered religious aspects were humbled when written down. And I will now demonstrate how they arrived at Yahweh or more traditionally "YHVH".

Going back to the legend I related earlier regarding Adam, this was a figure very precious to the Jews of those days. Adam is the Westernised name for the original AISH, as he was known in the earlier, unadulterated copies of Genesis. Please bear in mind the earlier comment that the Jewish language had no vowels, similarly they had no actual numbers, these were shown in the form of consonants, much the same as the Roman numeric system. The name AISH was sacred to the Jews, and therefore, to deprive the eyes of the profane, was ciphered numerically as 113. This ciphered number was then *humbled* or halved to 56.5. This humbling or halving has followed through to our times in the form of kneeling. As the Jews had not yet acquired the decimal system, it was actually written as 10 x 565. So, now you take these four numbers, i.e. 10, 5,6,5, and translate them back into letters, this is what you get. 10 is equivalent to the Jewish Yod or "Y", 5 is equivalent to "H", and 6 relates to "V" or "W". So you end up with "YHWH" or "YHVH". If you insert the vowels according to tradition and custom, you have "YAHWEH" or the more modern and traditional "JEHOVAH".

By giving this example I do not wish to imply that Jehovah was originally Adam, far from that, the complexities of the ancient Jewish system are far too involved for that simplistic conclusion. It is purely to demonstrate that there is far more to this aspect than meets the eye, and shows emphatically the rewards of research. The Jewish system of codifying anything that was sacred or specially unique to them, became almost a phobia among the scribes, and was constantly applied. This left future scholars to interpret the actualities as they saw fit, and is why you have so many valid and authoritative discourses on this complicated subject. For example, in explaining the theory of Jehovah's relationship to Adam, just put forward in my previously explained demonstration, to many scholars this is supported by the words:- "God created man in his own image", which they take to mean that, in the old Jewish sense, they are one and the same, as demonstrated in this codified numeric example! As you can well imagine, the theories on this particular aspect are literally endless, and I think that I have given enough for the moment.

Now I would like to draw your attention to one of the most important aspects of the H.R.A. ritual, that of the three Sojourners.

CHAPTER FOURTEEN

THE THREE SOJOURNERS

We three sojourners of Babylon are.

We are told that they are Master Masons from Babylon. One must assume that they are not Master Masons in our modern masonic sense, but are Master Masons in the traditional operative sense. Therefore they must have received their training and apprenticeships in Babylon, from their own people. From this we must deduce that there must have been a certain amount of freedom within their captivity for them to continue their traditional ways, and to pass them on to the new generations.

Clay tablets in various museums record inter alia, that the firm of Murashu & Sons had set up as Merchant bankers, Insurers, Estate Agents and building contractors. With Headquarters at Nippur the firm had branches throughout Mesopotamia and was a distinct commercial power in the land.

When the edict of Darius permitting resumption of the building of the Temple became known in Babylon, three young stone masons in the employ of Murashu and Sons resolved to go to Jerusalem and offer their services "in that great and glorious undertaking". It was known that during the interregnum many workmen had drifted away from the Temple site either to work on the land or on ordinary housing. Consequently our three sojourners set forth in high hopes.

The Master Masons continue to prove their heritage and status, and to demonstrate their disgust at those who remained behind for the purpose of tilling the land. This disgust, or scorn, registers a positive social distinction between the classes of people. Even though they are

Master Masons they are prepared to accept any lowly task as long as they can assist in rebuilding the Temple. Subsequently they are appointed to prepare the ground for the new foundations. With their basic tools they go on their way.

Having established that they must be operative Master Masons, with a good knowledge of buildings and their design and construction, they promptly proceed to remove the Archstone and the two keystones, the pivotal support for the dome or Arch, and then proceed to lower themselves into the vault below from the procured gap. They express their concern for what they might encounter once lowered, but show no concern whatsoever for the distinct probability of falling masonry, due to the removal of the main support stones. This ignorance shows a distinct lack of knowledge of architecture or, perhaps, once again, it is a bit of Masonic ritualistic licence.

All of the working tools and other various objects are very well covered in the three lectures and do not require any highlighting in this book, apart from perhaps a small reference to the five Platonic Bodies. These were created by Plato, the great philosopher and expert on the Ancient Mysteries, and a supposed participant in our Mystic Art. There are many references in Masonic Ritual to the "Ancient Mysteries", but there is no clear definition as to what they are, or where they come from. My researches have found them generally accepted to be of :- OSIRIS (Egypt), MITHRAS - (Persia), ADONIS - (Syria), DIONYSIS, BACCHUS and ELEUSIS - (Greece), DRUIDS - (Gaul and Britain). And are best summed in the words of PLATO:-

"The mysteries were established by men of great genius to teach purity, to ameliorate the cruelty of the Human

Race, to refine it's morals and manners and to restrain society by the obligations of Fraternity".

A better appraisal of the objectives of Freemasonry you would be pushed to find !!

Now let us look at that most sacred of all objects, the Altar of Incense.

We are taught, in the Craft, of the pious holiness of Hiram Abif, likewise that of Solomon and Hiram King of Tyre. We are also taught of the sacred sanctity of the Holy Ground, which no-one was allowed to walk upon, save the High Priest, and him, only once a year. In the middle of this Holy Ground, in the Holiest of Holies, stood the sacred pedestal or Altar of Incense, on the top of which was a plate of gold with the S.A.M.N.O.T.T.A.L.G.M.H. A Name so sacred and holy that no-one was allowed to mention it. YET, these three pious and holy men, felt it necessary to sign their names on it. Would not this be regarded as SACRILEGE?

CHAPTER FIFTEEN

COMPLETION BY NUMBERS

And now I would like to detail some more regarding the significance of numbers within the Jewish culture and religion. Although we refer to ourselves as companions, we could, legitimately call ourselves "Sherbangers", as in the phrase "The whole sherbang !" Which refers to "completeness." This completeness is very well demonstrated in this Supreme Degree and is synonymous with the number *seven*. This order is deemed as, although I have demonstrated my disagreement, the *completion* of the Third Degree in Craft Masonry, and is achieved after having taken *seven* steps. There are many other examples of seven indicating completeness, and I will quote but a few:-

- A Craft Master Mason completes his degree by 7 steps.
- King Solomon's Temple was completed in seven years.
- The world was completed in seven days.
- The seven ages of man completes a life.
- Seven days complete a week
- The seven colours complete a rainbow
- If you acquire knowledge from the seven pillars of wisdom your knowledge is deemed complete.
- In olden Jewish social law, no oath or promise was deemed of value or complete unless made in front of seven witnesses.
- Within the Holy Royal Arch ceremony the advance is completed by seven steps, halting and bowing at the 3rd, 5th and the 7th.

The examples given above complete the demonstration of the significance of seven and completeness.

And finally to show the connection of "Sherbangers or Sherbang" demonstrating "completeness".The word "Sherbang" (sic) *is* in some dialects the Jewish word for "Seven".

CHAPTER SIXTEEN

THE CONTINUANCE BY NUMBERS

I have earlier demonstrated the sacredness of the name JEHOVAH and how it is expressed in numerical form. The number 1 obviously refers to the single monotheistic God of the Jews. 2 refers to the spiritual duality that exists in everything. Good – Evil, Love – Hate, War – Peace, etc. 3 refers to the Trinity which is not exclusive to Christianity. The Jews have a trinity as represented by Joshua, Haggai and Zerubbabel in the Chapter namely: Priest, Prophet, King.

The number 3,5,& 7 are the manner in which the steps are taken when approaching the sacred altar, they are also the steps taken in the Craft degrees of Entered Apprentice,(3) Fellow Craft (5) and Master Mason (7).

And so it goes on. Another most important number for the Jews is 72. As the name of their God is too sacred to be tarnished by the human voice, and too sacred to be tarnished by the human hand by being written down, they have a certain number of attributes which they can use, depending in which context they wish to speak about their God, and yes there are 72 attributes in total. The most common and most frequently used are Adonai meaning Lord, El Shaddai meaning Lord Almighty. In Freemasonry we also use various soubriquets such as The Great Architect of the Universe, The Grand Geometrician of the Universe, The Most High etc. etc.

The Arms of the United Grand Lodge of England, which is emblazoned in gold on the front of the Book of Constitutions, and is carved in stone high up on the front of the prestigious building in Great Queen Street contains a phrase in Hebrew which we are told means "Holiness to the Lord", but in actual fact it translates literally to mean "Sacred to Jehovah." In the given meaning the word Lord replaces the replacement word Adonai, as the actual word of Jehovah should not be used, and this is sometimes used in a subtle manner to infer the Christian content of Freemasonry, as Jesus the Christian deity is so often referred to as Lord. If the use of the word Lord is used in this way and possibly for the purpose of encouraging Christianity within Freemasonry then why is it written just above the most sacred Jewish artifact, namely the Ark of the Covenant, why is the fish or cross of Calvary not represented? An unending question.

Keeping with the 72 theme, the Jewish Sanhedrin or Council of Elders is made up of 72 senior individuals. This is precisely why within the Exaltation ceremony the Candidate is told when he is given the Ensign of Judah, "…..*which you will ever have the right to bear unless 72 of the Elders are present*". This means that as a member of the Tribe of Judah, if one of the Elders is not present at the Council then you can attend and have a say. There is a particular reason for this positive jesture and instruction which is amply detailed in the exaltation ceremony.

When the Most Excellent inquires of the Principal Sojourner, in an attempt to establish their pedigree, "….. *but are you not descended from those who basely fled,….. or are you one of those who were left behind for the purpose of tilling the land?*" Both these possibilities are derogatory situations legitimately asked as many Jews either fled or remained behind in Babylon when the repatriation by Cyrus occurred. The indignant reply comes back, "…..*we would scorn to be descended from those who basely fled when the city was sorely oppressed, neither are we from those who were left behind for the purpose of tilling the land. Most Excellent, we are like yourselves, nobly born and members of your own tribes and families.....*" This clearly establishes them as members of the tribe of Judah and of the Royal line of David, so the banner under which they can reign must be the banner of Judah, and so it is this banner that the Candidate is handed. How many times have I asked within a Chapter that I have been lecturing at, "*Why is the Candidate given this particular Banner?*" How many times have I been given the answer..."*Because it is the nearest.*" The answer to this is.....countless times.

Having gone through the background and characters that make up the Supreme degree of the Holy Royal Arch now we must look at the ceremony itself.

CHAPTER SEVENTEEN

THE EXALTATION CEREMONY

The requirement is that you must be a Master Mason of four weeks and upwards before you can be Exalted into this Supreme degree. The word Exalted means "honoured" or "raised to higher rank".

You are tested on the strength of your qualification and then given a password which means "My people have found mercy". You are not told anymore about this password or of its origin, possibly because the person testing you and introducing you does not know its origin. The meaning only becomes apparent and significant if you ever get the opportunity of taking the "Passing of the Veils" or as it is properly called the Excellent Master degree. This lack of information is a shame as any information serves to aid a better understanding of what you are experiencing.

As a Candidate he should be prepared in his Master Masons regalia and should be slipshod as laid down in the Aldersgate book of ritual on page 39. So many Royal Arch Chapters do not observe this requirement, which I believe comes about through ignorance and a lack of understanding of the ritual. It is repeated several times throughout various Orders in Freemasonry, especially the Craft, that the High Priests of the Temple only walked on the Holy Ground and then only once a year when they made prayers of forgiveness for the apparent sins of the people. This ground was deemed so holy that no clothing or anything mundane should be allowed to make contact with it. At a most dramatic part of the Exaltation ceremony the Candidate is led blindfolded towards the most sacred and holy place and that piece of ground demands that the state of being slipshod be effected. After the usual Obligation the blindfold is removed and the sight presented at that moment is most profound for the Candidate, and is usually the moment most remembered, but is usually the moment least explained. The complete layout of the Temple is revealed in a most dramatic manner. The sight of the 12 ensigns of the Twelve Tribes of Israel held and displayed by the members of the Chapter, leaves a most lasting impression and which I have fully explained in an earlier part of this book.

The Candidate is then invited to retire and restore his personal comforts, *his footwear*, and on his return to the Chapter the ceremony is continued with. If the Candidate is not slipshod then the invitation for him to restore his personal comforts is superfluous and has no meaning.

The story of the Jewish people and their captivity in Babylon for 70 years is continued and the Candidate assists, in a most dramatic way, in the discovery of the long lost Master word which laid buried in darkness for 470 years ever since the death of Hiram Abiff, which specific event is portrayed in the Master Masons degree of the Craft. After the discovery of the long lost Master word you return, with those that assisted you, to the Sanhedrin, which is what the Chapter represents. This is a most interesting and revealing part of the Exaltation ceremony.

As a reward for the Candidate's efforts and discovery, he is then fully admitted to the Sanhedrin, which is the Jewish Council of Elders made up of 6 members from each of the 12 tribes of Israel, 72 in all. Then the Candidate is invested and formally welcomed as a Companion of the Order of the Holy Royal Arch Chapter of Jerusalem.

There then follows three Lectures, one given by each of the three Principals, that is Joshua,who delivers the Historical Lecture which is a retrospect on the Tabernacle erected by Moses, Aholiab and Bezaleel, and the Temple built by Solomon King of Israel, Hiram King of Tyre and Hiram Abiff. Lastly the Temple built by Zerubbabel, Haggai and Joshua.

The second Lecture is delivered by Haggai and is referred to as The Symbolical Lecture and details the forms, symbols and ornaments of a Royal Arch Chapter including the regalia, ensigns and banners that decorate the Chapter.

The Lectures are concluded with an oration by Zerubbabel called the Mystical Lecture and comprehends the forms and explanations of the signs and fully explains the origin and import of the long lost Master Word.

The Exhaltation Ceremony is a wonderful experience and a ceremony of enjoyment that educates and enthralls a worthy Candidate and I have kept my explanations of the actual ceremony to a minimum so as not to spoil any future enjoyment of this progressive step in Freemasonry.

After the ceremony has been enacted the conclusion is, as in all Masonic orders, completed by the investing of regalia and by pinning a breast jewel on the Candidate. This breast jewel consists mainly of the most common symbol throughout Freemasonry. I have asked many Freemasons, "what is the most common symbol within Freemasonry/", and the answer I always get is "the square and compasses" or even the Masonic Apron........ But the most common symbol within Freemasonry is the Star of David, otherwise known as the Seal of Solomon or to give it its proper name the Magen David. It appears on the flag of the Israelitish nation even to this day. Within our own Grand Lodge in London which contains many hundreds of doors, on either side there is a finger plate which has embossed very clearly this symbol. Most Masonic carpets are surrounded with this emblem. Every Companion of the Holy Royal Arch is permitted to wear his Royal Arch Jewel in a Craft Lodge, so you can see that the extent to which this symbol is displayed is quite prolific.

This symbol is very ancient and has been used in many cultures and belief systems, and to some small extent it still is, but how it came to be accepted and used as a distinctly Jewish symbol is quite fascinating. There are many speculations detailing the origins of its use and portrayal on the flag of Israel but I will only relate the one that has the greatest appeal for me. This paper was produced by Dr. Israel Shahak and is entitled "The Star of David"

In the year 1998 the modern State of Israel celebrated its fiftieth birthday. The Western world joined the celebration accordingly, including many practicing Christians. One could observe, especially in book stores, quantities of large Stars of David exhibited in the display windows as eye catchers in order to announce newly published books, which praise the history of the Zionist state. It is not the only point of criticism that Israel's history is explained rather one-sidedly in these books - especially by eliminating the fate of the eternal losers in the Middle East conflict, the Palestinians. Another critique deals with the fact that in western countries - fortunately - no one gets angry about advertisements using the Star of David, but that on the other hand public displays of Christian crucifixes in Israel will lead to violent protests and even measures by the legislation. This religious discrimination in Israel is not perceived outside of Israel, because the victims of the past are not allowed to be criticized today. The insight that it was the Catholic Order of the

Jesuits that selected the Star of David as a Jewish symbol is rather amusing, if not downright ironic.

Facts about the question how the Star of David evolved and how it was accepted by the Jews as "their" symbol are found only in contributions by good Israeli historians, published in specialized Israeli historical magazines. First of all it is necessary to realize that the Hebraic as well as the Yiddish name for this symbol is actually "Shield of David." I don't know why it was finally called "Star of David."

It should be noted that during antiquity and the Middle Ages the Jews possessed neither a national nor a religious symbol, even though various symbols were occasionally used, mostly the seven-armed chandelier (the official symbol of Israel) and the mounting lion.

The history of the Shield of David begins in Prague in the year 1648. During that last year of the Thirty Years War, Prague was besieged by the Swedish army. The town was mainly defended by Prague's citizens' militia, which included a Jewish unit. (This was the case until the days of Maria Theresa, who terminated the participation of Jews in the militia.) Because the Swedes did not succeed in taking the city, German Emperor Ferdinand III decided to assign honour flags and other decorations to all units of the citizens' militia in accordance with their self-defined affiliations. This included the Jews. However, no one in Vienna knew what kind of symbol to put on the flag, which was to be assigned to the Jews. Even the family Openhaimer, the emperor's "court Jews," did not know what to do. In their helplessness they turned to the scholarly Jesuits in Vienna to find a Jewish symbol. They finally came to the conclusion that King David "must have had the first and the last letter of his name, D, on his shield." They knew that the Jewish alphabet transformed towards Aramaic around the year *400 BC*, although the earlier alphabet was still used during festive occasions. Ancient Jewish coins, for example, are inscribed with these old letters, which are identical with the Punic letters. In this alphabet the letter *D* is a triangle, similar to today's Greek delta. Therefore they superimposed two triangles, which formed the Shield of David.

This was then embroidered on the Jewish flag and presented to the Jews of Prague as an honourable distinction for their duty for the country. The Jews in turn liked this symbol, and their scholarly rabbis understood its meaning, since the transformation of the Jewish alphabet was also

mentioned in the Talmud. So this new symbol began to spread to those towns, which had ties with Prague, and it was used in synagogues and during festive occasions. One of these towns was Frankfurt on Main, and when the Frankfurt family Rothschild was ennobled in the early nineteenth century, they placed this Jewish symbol, already famous at that time, on their coat of arms.

Since then the symbol has spread like wildfire to all Jewish communities, including the non-European especially because the Rothschild family had a considerable reputation among the Jews at that time. It was even reported in remote communities that the shield had magic powers, and there were stories, for example from Yemen, in which the ancestor of the Rothschild family

succeeded in exorcizing the devil from the emperor's daughter, etc. The Jews actually never heard of or used this symbol before the year *1648*, with the exception of the time between *700* and *400 BC*, when it was used by Jews as well as non-Jews in magic spells. In any case, it is rather amusing to know that the Jewish symbol, which is today on the flag of Israel, was actually given prominence by

Viennese Jesuits, as demanded by the German Emperor.

It is not maintained today in Israel that this symbol has an antique origin, because many Israelis are interested in Jewish history and are active as hobby archaeologists, and such an allegation would be quickly exposed as a lie. Therefore the origin of this symbol is simply ignored. Even the Zionist movement did not use the shield of David until the death of its founder Herzl; on Herzl's flag was the lion rampant, surrounded by seven five-pronged stars. However, David Wolfsohn, the successor of Herzl, who paid more attention to Jewish sensitivity, created the flag which later was accepted by the State of Israel. The white background with the blue bands at the edges correlates to today's Jewish prayer scarf. The colouring originates, however, from the Roman toga, where the violet was replaced with blue, as this special blue is a preferred Jewish colour for reasons unknown to me at this time.

It is written somewhere in the bible that God instructed Aaron, via Moses, to edge his garments with sky blue to distinguish him as an Elect Priest, hence our Craft Masonic Aprons come so designed and our Lodges and Chapters are dressed with the Star of David.

CHAPTER EIGHTEEN

CONCLUSION, & THE
JOURNEY CONTINUES

I cannot recomend enough a full study of this degree, its contained history of the Jewish nation at a most trying time of their development, namely their captivity by the Babylonians and 70 year stay in Babylon. Even the slightest of researches will yield a profit of understanding, and through that acquired understanding a much better delivery of the ritual as a participater in the conducting of the exaltation degree will be effected.

As detailed and emphasised in the Craft degrees, Freemasonry is a progressive science and therefore the further you go the more you will learn and subsequently understand. Remember that if you buy a book and only read chapter 1, that is all you will know and learn. You will know nothing about the following chapters and more importantly nothing of the final conclusion. Reading chapter 2 will yield a little further knowledge and possibly create a better understanding to chapter 1, but, again, little more will be forthcoming. As you may be aware there are many other Orders within Freemasonry that contain much more knowledge and information regarding the history of the Jewish nation and therefore greatly extend knowledge of the vitally important earlier degrees of the Craft and the Holy Royal Arch. With this in mind I feel that it would be pertinent to throw a little light on a couple of Masonic Orders that meet this important criteria in order that you, the reader, can decide if you wish to further your knowledge.

In a similar manner that the Order of Royal and Select Masters throws great light on the 3 Craft degrees and really details the relationship between Hiram Abiff and Adoniram, and consequently realises a greater understanding of those 3 Craft degrees which in turn produces a much better delivery of the ritual which stems from this greater understanding, so the Orders that I now highlight will realise a similar effect with the Holy Royal Arch.

The first Order that we should consider that is in direct connection to the Holy Royal Arch is the much talked about "Passing of the Veils" or to give its official title "The Excellent Master Degree".

This degree is regarded as the very important first step preceding actual exhaltation into the Holy Royal Arch, although not required under the English Constitution. Within Jewish religious history the inside of the Temple was hung with 4 different coloured veils symbolising various incidents of Jewish history up to that time. The Candidate passes through each veil with a sign and word for each reaching at last the final veil which then gives him the word and explanation that will gain him access into the Holy Royal Arch. That word is the key word that enables aspiring Candidates to gain admission into a Chapter under the English Constitution but unfortunately the history and significance of the word is not explained which in my opinion is a great shame as much is lost by its absence. Quite recently the Grand Council of the Royal and Select Masters agreed with the Supreme Grand Chapter of Scotland that they could again include the Excellent Master Degree as part of their Order but only as a degree of honour and reward to be bestowed on deserving aspirants of the Royal and Select Masters. This honour is currently only conferred within a Council of Thrice Illustrious Masters attached to a Provincial Royal and Select Masters. Currently each Province is allowed to recommend only 2 Candidates per Masonic year. This limited situation of availability means that the "migration" to Scotland to receive a life membership of a Scottish Chapter will continue, as this Passing the Veils degree is conferred automatically as part of the Chapter degree and is accepted under the English Constitution.

The next Order that I will highlight is The Knight Masons. This Order deals with the relationship between Zerubbabel and Cyrus the Great, also Zerubbabel's relationship afterwards with Darius.

These two very important relationships are lightly touched on within the Chapter ritual but very little is actually revealed. The qualification for joining is that you must be a Past Zerubbabel, and a member of the Allied Masonic Degrees, although not all constitutions enforce this requirement.

The Order consists of 3 degrees namely, Knight of the Sword, Knight of the East and Knight of the East and West. The ritual contains the full details of Zerubbabels important relationships and the manner in which assistance is enlisted and earned in helping to rebuild the Temple of Jerusalem. There are, at the moment, very few units that meet to conduct these fascinating degrees, but it is fast growing around the country.

The other Order is Pilgrim Preceptors, which details what happened after Titus razed the Temple to the ground in 70AD, as mentioned within the ritual of the Holy Royal Arch. After this tragic event many of the Jews fled to what they hoped would be safety in various parts of the world. Some found their way to Rome and continued their ceremonies in the catacombs of that city. Those catacombs are still to be seen to this very day and many tourists to the eternal city of Rome view them with awe and wonder. The Order of Pilgrim Preceptors is a system of 3 degrees, that of Pilgrim then Preceptor and finally the Chair degree of Illustrious Preceptor. The three degrees tell of the Jews holding their ceremonies within the catacombs and then seeking the co-operation of the Roman Emperor, which is granted to such an extent that he also becomes a member of their dedication, and finally how Christianity finally prevails from Judaism and finds its way to England through the auspices of St. Augustine.

As in the Chapter we celebrate the First and Holy Lodge, then the Second and Sacred Lodge, then the Third Grand and Royal Lodge, in Pilgrim Preceptors it is denominated the Fourth and Fraternal Lodge.The qualification for joining this wonderful Order is that you must be a Past Zerubbabel and display a Past "Z"s Jewel.

There are other Royal Arch related degrees that portray some incidents within Hebrew history and culture such as The Red Cross of Babylon conducted within an Allied Masonic Degree Council, but this is portrayed in much more detail within the Order of Knight Masons.

As in the Craft the ceremony and meeting is followed by the Festive Board within which there are a couple of aspects that I would like to explain. First there is a small catechetical exchange between the Most Excellent Zerubbabel and the Principal Sojourner that celebrates each of the three temples. After the commemoration of each temple the glass is raised and a drink is taken. This is effected with the left hand. This tradition has attracted many spurious and romantic explanations, but as I have mentioned before most often the simplest and most logical explanations are the ones that should enjoy the greatest acceptance. The explantion for drinking with the left hand that holds the most logic for me is that in the ancient past entry into the Chapter was restricted to Past Installed Masters of the Craft. Now if you consider the sign that demonstrates the penalty of a Past Installed Master you have a simple, logical and connected explanation for this left handed tradition.

Fairly recently it has been said that during the execution of "Chapter Fire" you should be pointing out horizontally with the index finger of your right hand. This cannot be right as you should be pointing downwards directly onto the Altar of Innocence which displays the 3 geometric signs which are animated during this exercise.

I trust that in this outlining and explanation of the Holy Royal Arch I have managed to bring you all something of interest and more, that I trust it will spur you into your own researches of this wonderful step in the progressive science of Freemasonry.

Ray Hudson
August 2014

Ray Hudson's First Best-Seller

SO YOU THINK YOU KNOW ABOUT FREEMASONRY?

Among Non-Masons, especially the sensationalist type, and even among many Freemasons, there are many misconceptions and misunderstandings of the original objectives, so much so that much of the meaning of Freemasonic ritual has become blurred and confused.

The original creators of this system of character building, social understanding, harmonising with your fellow man, and creating a better understanding of the individual's relationship with whatever he deems his God to be - and which eventually evolved into our Freemasonry as practised today - were very intelligent individuals. They possessed a deliberate intent regarding the most suitable method of encouraging others to achieve these high objectives. By this system of progression of serious (but most enjoyable) enactments based upon either biblical or events in recognised history, it was hoped that man's understanding of himself and his God would lead eventually to peaceful harmony throughout life.

So great was its objectives and construction that it received many imitators, some not quite achieving the ideals set by the original creators. But others have managed to take the original objectives a little further - hence we have many Orders within Freemasonry, thereby confirming the progressive nature of the system.

This book is an attempt to "get back to basics", and will hopefully bring some additional light upon what I consider the greatest method of self-improvement ever devised by man. In saying this I give due respect to the diverse spiritual and mystical systems of the world's many cultures; but they appear to me to be specific for those so inclined, whereas Freemasonry appeals and satisfies on many levels.

Ray Hudson

PARCHMENT BOOKS is committed to publishing high quality Esoteric/Mystic classic texts at a reasonable price.

With the premium on space in modern dwellings, we also strive - within the limits of good book design - to make our products as slender as possible, allowing more books to be fitted into a given bookshelf area.

Parchment Books is an imprint of Aziloth Books, which has established itself as a publisher boasting a diverse list of powerful, quality titles, including novels of flair and originality, and factual publications on controversial issues that have not found a home in the rather staid and politically-correct atmosphere of many publishing houses.

Titles Include:

Stellar Mythology & Masonic Astronomy	Robert Hewitt Brown
Secret Doctrines of the Rosicrucians	Magus Incognito
Corpus Hermeticum	G.RS. Mead (trans.)
Esoteric Buddhism	A.P. Sinnett
The Virgin of the World	Hermes Trismegistus
Raja Yoga	Yogi Ramacharaka
Knowledge of the Higher Worlds	Rudolf Steiner
The Most Holy Trinosophia	St Germaine
The Mystical Qabalah	Dion Fortune
The Gospel of Thomas	Anonymous
Pistis Sophia	G.R.S. Mead (trans.)
Q.B.L. or, The Bride's Reception	Frater Achad
The Lord of the World	René Guénon
Shambala the Resplendent	Nicholas Roerich
The Teachings of Zoroaster	Shapurji A. Kapadia
Moses and Monotheism	Sigmund Freud

Obtainable at all good online and local bookstores.
View Aziloth's full list at: www.azilothbooks.com

We are a small, approachable company and would love to hear any of your comments and suggestions on our plans, products, or indeed on absolutely anything. Aziloth is also interested in hearing from aspiring authors whom we might publish. We look forward to meeting you.
Contact us at: info@azilothbooks.com.

CATHEDRAL CLASSICS

Parchment Book's sister imprint, Cathedral Classics, hosts an array of classic literature, from ancient tomes to twentieth-century masterpieces, all of which deserve a place in your home. A small selection is detailed below:

Mary Shelley	*Frankenstein*
H G Wells	*The Time Machine; The Invisible Man*
Niccolo Machiavelli	*The Prince*
Omar Khayyam	*The Rubaiyat of Omar Khayyam*
Joseph Conrad	*Heart of Darkness; The Secret Agent*
Jane Austen	*Persuasion; Northanger Abbey*
Oscar Wilde	*The Picture of Dorian Gray*
Voltaire	*Candide*
Bulwer Lytton	*The Coming Race*
Arthur Conan Doyle	*The Adventures of Sherlock Holmes*
John Buchan	*The Thirty-Nine Steps*
Friedrich Nietzsche	*Beyond Good and Evil*
Henry James	*Washington Square*
Stephen Crane	*The Red Badge of Courage*
Ralph Waldo Emmerson	*Self-Reliance, & Other Essays (series1&2)*
Sun Tzu	*The Art of War*
Charles Dickens	*A Christmas Carol*
Fyodor Dostoyevsky	*The Gambler; The Double*
Virginia Wolf	*To the Lighthouse; Mrs Dalloway*
Johann W Goethe	*The Sorrows of Young Werther*
Walt Whitman	*Leaves of Grass - 1855 edition*
Confucius	*Analects*
Anonymous	*Beowulf*
Anne Bronte	*Agnes Grey*
More	*Utopia*

full list at: www.azilothbooks.com

Obtainable at all good online and local bookstores.

Lightning Source UK Ltd.
Milton Keynes UK
UKOW05f1002160315

247943UK00001B/4/P